CW00683855

A

DESCRIPTION AND EXPLANATION OF THE METHOD
OF PERFORMING

# POST-MORTEM EXAMINATIONS

IN THE DEAD-HOUSE OF

## THE BERLIN CHARITÉ HOSPITAL,

WITH

*ESPECIAL REFERENCE TO MEDICO-LEGAL*

BY

## PROFESSOR RUDOLPH VIRCHOW.

*Translated from the Second German Edition by*
Dr. T. P. SMITH.

LONDON:
J. & A. CHURCHILL, NEW BURLINGTON STREET.
—
1880.

# TRANSLATOR'S PREFACE.

In the following work Prof. Virchow gives some account
of his early experience as Prosector in the dead-house of
the Berlin Charité Hospital, and traces the subsequent
development, under his auspices, of a systematic method
of conducting post-mortem examinations. He also
criticises, explains, and illustrates the regulations which
have been promulgated throughout Germany for the
guidance of medical jurists in performing autopsies and
drawing up reports. (Regulativ für das Verfahren der
Gerichtsärzte bei den gerichtlichen Untersuchungen
menschlicher Leichname. Herausgegeben von der Königl.
wissenschaftlichen Deputation für das Medicinalwesen,
Januar. 6, 1875.) He also gives four interesting cases in
which the post-mortem examinations were performed by
himself, the order of sequence enjoined by the regulations
being closely adhered to. An examination of these cases
will show that nothing has been omitted which could
throw any possible light on the cause of death. They
may be taken as examples of the way in which all
post-mortem examinations for medico-legal purposes

should be conducted. Lest the length of the notes should seem excessive, Prof. Virchow expressly states that three hours are sufficient even for complicated cases. It will be obvious, on referring to the details, that only by following out a systematic plan could a thoroughly complete examination be performed in that time. Such an examination, however, would be infinitely more satisfactory than one in which important points were overlooked, and discovered only on subsequent investigation. It is much to be wished that a method similar to the one which has received the high sanction of Prof. Virchow were adopted in this country.

In this second edition a fourth case has been added, with a commentary, and some explanatory remarks on the method of opening the thorax. The volume is still further improved by the addition of four plates, illustrating Prof. Virchow's method of opening the heart and thorax. The German Government Regulations for the guidance of medical jurists in performing post-mortem examinations for legal purposes are given in an appendix.

REIGATE, *December*, 1879.

# CONTENTS.

———◦◦———

# METHOD OF PERFORMING POST-MORTEM EXAMINATIONS.

On taking up my appointment, in the year 1844, as assistant to Robert Froriep, the Prosector at the Charité, I found that the autopsies were at that time somewhat irregularly and unmethodically performed. The Prosector himself made but few examinations, and these only by special requisition; the greater number were performed, without any technical plan, by the Charité surgeons—young medical men, subsequently styled "assistants," who had not yet passed the State examination. No minutes of the proceedings were made at the time, and only when the examination was over were notes taken down from memory. Froriep himself but very rarely gave a course on post-mortem examinations; he did so only once during my experience. Notwithstanding his eminent scientific attainments and his great manual dexterity (perhaps, indeed, on account of these his qualifications—at any rate, as a consequence of their limited practical employment), there was but little thoroughness in Froriep's method; in many respects,

B

indeed, it was so ill adapted for the purpose, that it was a matter of difficulty to make any discoveries by its means.

Thus, to take only one example, it was his custom, when examining the spinal cord, to divide it longitudinally, from before or behind, by one long straight cut, and to dissect it in two equal lateral halves. This certainly made a very elegant section, and to do it properly required practice and care; but, however well it was performed, there were but very few cases in which it was of any use. The natural consequence was that Froriep's attention was directed principally to the membranes and roots of the nerves, and that the commonest and most important alterations in the white substance remained unnoticed.

I therefore had a double task to perform, especially after I became Prosector in 1846. On the one hand, I aimed at causing the autopsies to be made by one person, at introducing a system of regular note-taking, and of collecting these notes in order to obtain a useful series of reports. This was a matter of no great difficulty, after many startling incidents had shown how thoroughly erroneous were the results obtained in the absence of technical skill. It very soon happened that every clinical teacher and class-director became interested in the fact that the post-mortem examinations were made by my hand. When, in the year 1849, I accepted the call to Würzburg, I left behind me a large collection of reliable reports. Unfortunately, only a few fragments of these were forthcoming when I was recalled to the Charité in 1856.

On the other hand, it was necessary to discover a regular method for pathologico-anatomical investigation, and to introduce a definite employment of technical terms, which could be adhered to as a rule for all ordinary cases. Such a method I have perfected as years have rolled on, and it has now been sufficiently long in use for its value to have been tested by experience. It has naturally been formed into shape from a double point of view. The first require-ment was that it should permit of the most complete insight possible into the extent of the alterations in every organ; and, in the second place, in order to provide for a distinct demonstration adapted for educational purposes, such an arrangement was necessary as would cause the least possible disturbance in the connection of the parts examined. There were therefore these two problems, to some extent opposed to each other. They have nevertheless been solved in a satisfactory manner.

I have at present no intention of discussing this method in all its details. This has been done, to a certain extent, in the recent regulations drawn up, for the guidance of the medical jurist when making autopsies for legal purposes, by the Royal Committee of Science for Medical Affairs, under date of January 6 of this year (1875), and confirmed by the Minister of the Ecclesiastical, Educational, and Medical Departments, under date February 13 of the same year, and which are appended to this work.

It is true that these regulations do not correspond in all particulars with our system. This depends, in part, upon the difference in the nature of the tasks—which, for example, is very striking in every step of the external inspection, this latter being far more important for the medical jurist than for the pathological anatomist. Another point is that it has been thought expedient in the deliberations of the Committee to make certain alterations, which permit of a more simple and rapid manipulation of those organs which are less important for legal purposes. Taken as a whole, the regulations are invariably an expression of the knowledge, acquired through long experience, of the most suitable arrangements for conducting post-mortem examinations.

The necessity for superseding the old rules of November 15, 1858, had gradually become very urgent. Strictly speaking, these were already antiquated at the time of their issue. They had no sooner appeared than I pointed out their defects, and drew particular attention to the necessity of insisting—in autopsies for medico-legal pur-

poses, as in everything else now—upon completeness of
examination and exactness of method, both in the investigation and in note-taking, so that it might be decided—
subsequently, though not in anticipation—whether there
was any significance or importance in what was observed,
or whether it was accidental and unessential.—(*Deutsche
Klinik*, 1859, No. 2.) There was, in truth, even at that
time, no difference of opinion on these points. The regulations certainly continued in force for fifteen years; this,
however, is accounted for not merely by the legitimate bias
of the authorities against too frequent changes, but still
more so by the recognition of the fact that, before making
demands, which, in no trifling degree, exceeded the limits
of that amount of technical medical training which had
previously been deemed sufficient, it would be necessary
first to train a larger number of well-educated medical
jurists. This held good not merely with regard to the
microscopical examination necessary in so many cases, but
even with reference to the ordinary anatomical techni-
calities of post-mortem examinations.

So long ago as 1859 I indicated in my lectures the
direction which the change should take. I then stated as
follows:— "The present generation is conversant with
pathological anatomy only as a supplement of the clinic.
As a rule, the clinical teacher determined while the patient
was alive which organ was to be the object of investigation;
and the autopsy likewise was usually confined to that
organ, or at least dealt with all the others only in a
secondary manner. The clinical anamnesis consequently
decided the course of the anatomical examination. We all
know what was the result. The fact is that we can further
the advance of medical science in the most essential manner
by acquiring the habit of submitting all the other organs of
the body to a minute examination; for it is obvious that
we can do as much by anatomical as by clinical examination." I ought, indeed, perhaps to have said that we have
to do more by anatomical than by clinical observation, for

the one reason that the anatomical examination must be completed once for all, and does not admit of repetition; whereas we can at the bedside, as a rule, return again and again to the same case, and if any omission has occurred in one examination, it can be remedied in the next or a subsequent one. But, irrespective of this, there is a great difference between being able to get directly at an internal organ and examine it in every particular, and having to content ourselves with following out and realising certain symptoms.

Medico-legal technics—with all due deference to the independence of forensic medicine—will, however, always go hand-in-hand with pathological anatomy; for this latter is the more universal: it has to deal with cases of all kinds, and for that reason is a great protection against that one-sidedness with which medico-legal practice is so much encumbered. As a matter of fact, it must be conceded that the great majority of medico-legal reports have exhibited such an astonishing sameness, even in their phraseology; such a very peculiar style, nowhere else to be found; such a want of real objectivity, that it was an extremely tedious business to read through any number of them consecutively. There was such an amount of similarity among many of them that it might have been thought that they all referred to the same case.

The number of better educated physicians has gradually increased. The new examination for the North German Bund, and more recently for the German Empire, recognises pathological anatomy as a special subject, and also tests the candidates in pathological histology. A more intimate knowledge of pathologico-anatomical technics and microscopical manipulation has been thereby introduced; and it was therefore high time, considering that the examination rules of September 25, 1869, had now been six years in force, to lay down similar directions for the forensic examination, and afterwards to institute regulations for conducting autopsies for medico-legal purposes. This has now been done, and it is to be hoped that the innovation will prove very beneficial, and promote the efficacy of the laws; for a not insignificant portion of the administration of the criminal law is entirely dependent upon a correct and objective examination on the part of the medical jurist.

Experience, indeed, teaches us that the great majority of cases in which the Courts are compelled to appeal for advice to the Medical Colleges and to the Committee of Science for Medical Affairs, refer to those autopsies in which either the examination or the note-taking has been so irregularly performed that the nature of the case still remains ambiguous. It would, I am sure, be a matter of no difficulty to collect a great number of examples in which the faulty performance of the autopsy has rendered obscure cases in themselves clear and simple, and has made unintelligible those which were at all ambiguous. This observation explains the increasing number of the revision remarks, which are so complained of by many physicians, and also the necessity for inserting many detailed directions—perfectly obvious, but not always attended to—in the regulations for the due performance of autopsies. The revision remarks having been brought to the cognisance of the State Attorney and the Court, the prosecution of an accused person can be resumed; this, for a long time, had not been possible, owing to faulty examinations and the very arbitrary opinions expressed by those who performed them.

After such experiences, which, considering the evidence obtained in the medical examinations with reference to the ordinary way in which cases are investigated and observed, may easily extend in various other directions, the practical necessity of laying down strict rules appeared quite imperative. In like manner, there could be no doubt that, for educational purposes, and for the majority of ordinary cases, a methodical procedure in post-mortem examinations presupposes the establishment of a definite plan.

It is scarcely necessary to point out that there are many *cases in which* deviations from this method are not merely allowable, but also absolutely necessary. The individuality of the case must often determine the plan of the examination. But we must not begin with individualising, nor make a rule of the exceptions. The expert may allow himself to make alterations, supposing they are well grounded, but he must be able to remember his motive for so doing, and also to state it.

For this purpose, however, a full and intimate acquaintance with the reasons why the plan or rule has been laid down is quite imperative. The method should be practised, not mechanically, but systematically, as it has for its basis well-weighed experience, and not mere casual observations. He who is conversant with these reasons will also be able to judge of their correctness, and of the occasions when a departure from the rule is indicated. Thus the rule will be that when the cranial cavity is opened, the exposed parts—viz., the dura mater, the great longitudinal sinus, the pia mater, the surface of the cerebral hemispheres— must be first examined, and described in succession. But if the dura mater is adherent to the skull-cap, the best plan is to divide the former before forcibly detaching the latter, and to remove the skull-cap with the dura mater adhering to it; for if long and violent attempts be made to separate the skull-cap from the still closed and adherent dura mater, this latter usually gets torn, the brain itself crushed, and the parts so altered that sometimes their original condition is quite undiscoverable. In new-born infants and in children these parts are, as a rule, adherent ; so that in these young subjects, if we wish to avoid the risk of converting the brain into a mass of pulp, we must make an alteration in the method adapted for examining adult cases. But if these adhesions are found in adults as individual appearances in exceptional cases, we must also in such cases make an alteration in the method to be pursued.

In a systematic and scientific performance of an autopsy nothing is more difficult, and at the same time more important, than the insight into the reasons for pursuing a definite order of sequence in every detail of the examination. Let us therefore consider this point somewhat minutely. The course of the examination is generally dependent upon the order of succession. If for ordinary cases we require a definite process and a prescribed order, we do so not merely because such an arrangement is the surest guarantee for the completeness of the examination, and the best preventive against omitting important parts, but for the still greater reason that an unmethodical plan is the greatest possible obstacle to the subsequent collection of valuable reports. An unmethodical examination artificially and prematurely obliterates the existent condition of the parts.

Let us take a few examples. In many examinations the position of the diaphragm is of the greatest importance. This, generally speaking, cannot be determined if we open the thorax before the abdomen, or even at the same time; or if, after first opening the abdomen, we do not examine the diaphragm before opening the thorax. In former times, when the physicians allowed the assistants to make the post-mortem examinations, the custom was almost universal for a dissecting-room servant to open the thorax and abdomen before the arrival of the medical staff. The object was to save time and trouble. It soon became evident in forensic practice that such a proceeding as this made it impossible to define exactly the state of the thorax and its contents. In new-born children especially, it is necessary to ascertain carefully the position of the diaphragm, because in them the main question hinges upon the establishment of respiration; and not merely this, but the extent to which respiration has been carried is the important point. On this account the direction was that the abdomen should be opened first. The regulation of 1858 was in this respect quite correct. Section 17, a, ran as follows:—"After the abdomen has been opened, the position of the diaphragm is to be noted with reference to the corresponding ribs; and to ascertain this correctly in new-born children the abdomen should be opened first, and subsequently the thorax and head." Unfortunately, this very proper direction was made obscure by the words immediately preceding it. They ran thus:—" The respiration test must now be commenced, and for this purpose, (a) after the abdomen has been opened," etc. This preface was altogether out of place, for we do not determine the position of the diaphragm with a view to the respiration test, but both are co-ordinate means for establishing the fact that respiration has been performed. Still worse, however, was the ambiguity involved in the choice of the expression "opening." Taken by itself the word is not synonymous with "dissection," but the medical jurists made use of "opening" in the sense of "dissection," and instead of opening and dissecting the thorax immediately after opening the abdomen and determining the position of the diaphragm, they finished the dissection of the abdomen before they even opened the thorax. Indeed, this bad practice was so universal, that even when, as occasionally happened, a more enlightened physician examined the thorax first, and then dissected the abdomen, he was blamed for so doing by the medical boards in their revision reports.

What, however, is the consequence of thus first dissecting the abdomen? I will assume that in the removal of the spleen, the stomach, and the liver, the diaphragm has not been cut, although this indeed frequently happens; but on cutting through the veins of the liver (in removing this organ), and on opening, as particularly directed, the inferior vena cava, it is impossible to prevent the blood escaping partially or, if not coagulated, completely from the right auricle through the large venous trunks which have been opened. If, after this has been done, the thorax be examined, it is quite possible that the right auricle and the right side of the heart may be found collapsed and containing little or no blood, in cases where proper examination would have revealed an entirely opposite state of things. How often it happens that the report is, in consequence, very different from what it ought to be, and the opinion based thereon also falsified!

For this reason the new regulation directs, what I have for years taught, that, under all circumstances, the abdomen is to be first opened, but not dissected. It is only necessary in this stage to determine the position of the diaphragm, as well as that of the organs, any abnormal contents of the abdomen which may possibly be present, and the colour of the parts exposed. Then the thorax is immediately to be examined, unless there is some cogent reason for departing from the rule. The suspicion of poisoning is always admitted to be a reason of this nature, as in this case the whole of the examination centres in the stomach; and every precaution must be taken to place it and its contents, without loss or change, at the disposal of the law.

The regulation that, as a rule, the dissection of the abdomen is to follow that of the thorax, but, on the other hand, that the abdomen is to be opened, and its general state determined before the opening of the thorax, has necessitated, in the new regulations, the altering of certain directions referring to the minutes of examinations. It is to be hoped that medical jurists will readily familiarise themselves with these changes, and it is not necessary further to allude to them. On the other hand, it appears to me that it is not superfluous to explain why it is that we ought to determine the general condition of the abdominal organs before opening the thorax. In reference to this, the new regulations order as follows, in section 18, para. 2:—"In addition to this, the position, colour, and other appearances presented by the exposed intestines, and also the occurrence of any abnormal contents, are next to be specified, and the position of the diaphragm to be determined by examining it with the hand."

It is evident that the position of the abdominal viscera cannot be exactly determined after the thorax has been *opened and the anterior attachments of the diaphragm to a* great extent divided. The further the examination of the thorax proceeds, the more numerous the organs which are removed, and the more freely the connections between the diaphragm and parts of the thorax are divided, the looser does this muscle become, and the greater the displacement of the abdominal viscera towards the thoracic cavity. A further examination may reveal something previously unnoticed, and necessitating a comparison between the position of the abdominal viscera and injuries of the abdominal walls, and we may wish to examine thoroughly the relations to each other of two of the abdominal viscera; but the previous opening of the thorax will render all such attempts nugatory. I need only mention those by no means rare cases in which incipient peritonitis is discovered, and where it becomes necessary to ascertain whether the peritonitis was caused by injury or was due to a pathological process in any one of the abdominal viscera. In a case where the spot which exhibits the signs of a limited peritonitis is not exposed when the abdomen is opened, it will scarcely be possible to determine the causal connection if the position of the viscera has been much disturbed before the spot has been discovered.

With regard to the *colour* of the abdominal viscera, we must especially bear in mind that the notion is even now very prevalent that arterial blood, and therefore the arterial vessels, in the dead body as in the living, are distinguishable by their deep-red (*hochroth*) or bright-red (*hellroth*) colour. This notion is founded on a primary error. Arterial blood in a dead body is always of a dusky-red colour. This is just as true with regard to the blood of the pulmonary veins and left side of the heart as to that of the aorta and peripheral arteries. Any one who has carefully noticed the large arteries on the base of the brain, which, on account of their relatively free and superficial course, are very convenient for observation; any one who has been impressed with their bluish-red, thoroughly venous appearance; any one who has carefully

observed in the left auricle the dusky-red blood which has
just come from the lungs and just been aërated, and this
in persons who have not died from suffocation,—ought for
ever to be cured of the mistake of supposing that a dead
body contains bright-red arterial blood.    No recently
exposed portion of a dead body has a bright-red colour ; the
lung certainly may form an exception to this statement, but
only when filled with air, in which case, even after death,
a certain quantity of oxygen may be absorbed.    And even
in the lung this is not usually the case to the extent supposed.    In this organ the tissue containing the blood is
full of alveoli containing air, and thus, as when froth is
formed, a whitish colour is produced, which, mixed with
dusky-red, produces a bright-red shade.    This is beauti-
fully seen in the lungs of new-born children.

It follows, as a matter of course, and in individual cases
it can be directly proved, that in no portion of the viscera
of a dead body can arterial injection be recognised by the
colour test.    Even when the arterial injection is very considerable, the colour of the part may be just as bluish-red
or blackish-red as in venous hyperæmia.    Whoever wishes
to assure himself on this point may do so by examining the
kidneys, where, with the naked eye or with a simple lens,
he will easily see the Malpighian corpuscles, purely arterial
structures, appearing as very dark-red points or granules
in consequence of the fulness of their vessels.

After death, however, the blood does not lose its power
of absorbing oxygen, and of thereby assuming an arterial
appearance—i.e., a deep-red colour.    This statement, indeed,
must be taken with certain limitations, for there are some
cases in which the blood, even before death, possesses a
much diminished power of absorbing oxygen, and there
are others in which it becomes so altered after death that
its capacity in this respect is entirely lost.    In both cases
it is, however, arterial blood.    On the other hand, even in
ordinary cases, venous blood in the dead body possesses the
power of absorbing oxygen.    Thus it may happen that a

part affected with venous hyperæmia becomes, when exposed to the air, after a time, deep-red in colour, and exhibits the appearance of an arterial injection. Naturally the change takes place much less readily and quickly in large and very full veins than in small ones; it is therefore of most frequent occurrence in the plexuses formed by the venous radicles.

What a great number of erroneous judgments have been due to want of knowledge of these very simple facts! How often has irritation or even inflammation been inferred merely because of a deep-red colour of the parts, or of a deep-red injection of the small vessels, whereas this coloration has really arisen in the course of the dissection! For the time usually required for the examination of the thoracic organs is amply sufficient for the change, from dark-red to bright-red, to take place in those viscera of the abdomen which have been exposed. Hence the requirement in the regulations that the colour of the exposed portions of the abdomen is to be determined directly the cavity has been opened—that is, before the oxygen of the air that has gained access has had time to exert its influence.

As I have just touched upon this subject, I may say a few words more with reference to the much misused term, "fulness of the vessels." With regard to this, it appears to me important, considering the only too frequent incidents impressed on my memory, to lay great stress on the following points:—

1. Capillary injection cannot be recognised as such, in a general way, with the naked eye. The finest vascular network which the naked eye is able to discriminate is either arterial or venous, and in the majority of cases, venous. This holds good especially of mucous membranes, in which the comparatively superficial position of the venous radicles very frequently causes them to be mistaken for capillaries. All capillaries are microscopic objects, and when filled with blood it is not red capillaries but red tissue which is

observable. This redness really gleams out from the
interior of the tissue, and we can here, in a certain sense,
justly say that the tissue is injected. Nowhere can this
condition be so well observed as in the cerebral substance,
especially in the soft, translucent grey matter. All shades,
from the faintest reddish tinge up to a dark hydrangea-
red, are here met with, and though single fine vessels filled
with blood may be distinguished in the red spots, we can
easily demonstrate that the colour of the tissue is not due
to these vessels. To this category belongs that peculiar
mottled redness which is not unfrequently found in the
white medullary substance and in the optic thalamus and
corpus striatum, and which is very similar to the first
symptom of frost-redness on the surface of the body. In
my " Cellular Pathology" (fourth edition, page 107, Fig. 35)
I have given an illustration of such a condition; it can
easily be understood from this; only the few larger vessels,
which are shown in the drawing, could with difficulty be
made out with a lens; all the other vessels were only visible
on careful examination with the microscope. It is, therefore,
intelligible that to an expert there is something absurd in
the expression " inflammatory hyperæmia " (occurring as it
does in numerous reports) referring to anything which can
be directly discovered with the naked eye. Nowhere is
this expression more absurd than when it is used in reference to the stomach, as it can be proved in the majority of
the reports that what the observer has noticed have only
been veins.

2. The venous or arterial character of a vessel is never to
be determined by the quality of the blood therein contained; but in all cases we must be guided only by its
structure, its connections, and its position. In other words,
it is not to be discovered at the autopsy whether a vessel
is an artery or a vein; but, with regard at least to all
larger vessels, this ought to be known previously. It is
true, that it once occurred to me that a practising phy-

sician, who presented himself for examination, was very much astonished when (in consequence of various wrong answers) I asked him a question as to the nature of some of the larger vessels of the brain. His answer was, that he had not prepared himself on that subject, because he had not expected to be asked any questions, in this examination, in normal anatomy. However, I think I can maintain the proposition, that, inasmuch as without a correct knowledge of angiology, and even of the smaller vessels, the results of a medico-legal investigation may so easily be false, no one can possibly be a good medical jurist who is is not thoroughly conversant with these matters. In referring especially to medical jurists, I do not, of course, mean to imply that such knowledge ought not to be possessed by ordinary physicians; but what I wish to express is, that it is still more obligatory in the former class. In puzzling cases (which, I admit, do occur to the expert, and even to the anatomist) there is one plan which will be found to be of the greatest assistance, and that is to follow the course of the vessel until a point is reached where the size becomes a sufficient guide as to its nature, even to the less experienced observers; and particularly if in a membrane we meet with a smaller vessel filled with blood, we can, by displacing the blood, often succeed in ascertaining the course and connection of the vessel.

3. A statement with reference to the quantity of blood contained in a part can be regarded as approximatively exact only when the description indicates not merely the kind of vessels in which the blood is contained, but also, to some extent, the degree of their fulness. By this I do not assert that we are able without minute examination—which is not in all cases possible—to make such statements with regard to all parts; and with reference to many of them, I confess that a general description of their appearance and colour is all that is required. This holds good, for example, of the spleen, with regard to which no one,

by simply looking at the surface of a section, could properly estimate which of the small vessels were filled, and the extent of their fulness. But there are many parts of the body—and this refers especially to the mucous and serous membranes; consequently, to the majority of the internal surfaces—which can very easily be examined, and in which, in important cases, the attempt should always be made to ascertain positively the nature of the vessels concerned. It is certainly easier to pronounce an opinion than to give such a description; but the experience of the slight utility of such opinions has caused the Committee of Sciences to include the following direction in their new Regulations, section 28, para. 5.

" In all cases a statement must be given with reference to the amount of blood contained in each important part ; and what is required is a terse description, not merely an opinion couched in such terms as ' profuse,' ' moderate,' ' slight,' ' much reddened,' ' full of blood,' ' bloodless,' etc."

This explanation may suffice to illustrate the way in which statements should be made with reference to the colour of the exposed abdominal viscera, and to what extent it is important that this should be determined immediately after the abdomen is opened. I will only make one more remark—that every manipulation of the intestines and other parts of the abdomen, by which their position is altered, their mutual pressure diminished or increased, or even any direct pressure with the hand, alters the amount of blood contained, and not only of this, but also of the gaseous, fluid, or more solid matter contained in separate portions of the intestines.

Still more important than the determination of the colour is the immediate ascertaining of any foreign substance which the abdomen may happen to contain. If there be gas, it is very obvious that its existence can be generally proved only at the moment of opening the abdomen. If it be a liquid, there is the danger of losing some of it unless it be collected at once. In every case, however, when the thorax is opened and its contents removed, it is almost impossible to prevent blood and other fluids from getting into the abdomen; and thus, when this latter cavity is examined, the appearances are obscured or directly falsified. The like holds good of those cases in which the subsequent examination has particularly to be directed not to the thorax, but to single parts of the abdomen; for example, the stomach. It is extremely difficult, in removing and opening this organ, to avoid soiling the abdomen; and therefore, if the existence or non-existence of any anomalous contents has not been previously determined, it is scarcely possible to do this after the stomach has been interfered with.

I can be much more brief in my remarks with regard to the first portion of the examination of the thorax. Nevertheless, clear as the conditions are, I know from manifold experience how difficult it is to arrange a definite method of procedure. In explanation, I must first make the apparently paradoxical remark that "thorax," strictly speaking, is quite an abstract term. In reality, there is nothing which corresponds to it except in the skeleton, or in a cadaver from which the viscera have been removed. In the living subject and in the ordinary condition of a dead body there is not one, but several, thoracic cavities. For there are, in the first place, two quite separate pleural sacs, and therefore also pleural cavities; and, in the next place, a pericardium, and in it a pericardial cavity.

Therefore in a dead body we never really open the "thoracic cavity," but rather, if in removing the breast-bone we do not somewhat awkwardly cut and "open" the pericardium as well, the result is that when the sternum, together with the cartilages of the ribs, has been detached, we come on each side into a pleural cavity or space. The so-called mediastinum is no cavity in this sense, but a septum filled with loose tissue, and it would be far more intelligible if we represented the mediastinum as a septum, and did not speak of it as a space. As, therefore, in open-

ing the thoracic cavity we really come into the pleura
sacs, our duty is here, as in the abdomen, immediately t
examine both these sacs with regard to the position, colour
etc., of their contents, and also to look very particularl'
for any possible foreign body which may be present.    Thi
examination is much more important here than in th
abdomen, for it happens only too often that in cuttin¿
through the first rib and the sterno-clavicular articulation
as well as in the actual removal of the sternum, large vein
(such as the internal mammary, the internal jugular, anc
the innominate) are pierced, cut, or torn, and fluid o
coagulated blood escapes.    In a short time this finds it
way into one or even both of the pleural sacs, and, n
matter whether these previously contained anything or not
it is subsequently impossible to express a positive opinion
either as regards the quantity or the quality, or in man}
cases even to decide as to the pre-existence, of any con·
tents whatever.    I need not explain how very importan·
the demonstration of any anomalous contents in one o¡
both pleural sacs may be in helping us to form an opinio¡
with regard to a case, and I therefore think that it is cer·
tainly proper always to commence the examination of th¢
thoracic cavity by ascertaining the condition of the pleura·
sacs, and to leave the lungs and the pericardium for sub·
sequent observation. For he who would open the pericardium
and dissect the heart before determining whether hæmato·
thorax or hydrothorax or pleuritis be present, is a man who
ought not to undertake a post-mortem examination at all.

But it is just as evident that the lungs ought not to be
removed from the thorax before the heart has been
examined, for this cannot be done without separating the
pulmonary artery and veins.    Unless ligatures are previously applied to these vessels—and it is neither cus-
tomary nor needful so to do—their division will be
immediately followed by the escape of a certain amount
of the contents of the left auricle, of the trunk of the
pulmonary artery, and of the right ventricle ; and just the

same thing happens as when we remove the liver and open the inferior vena cava before opening the thorax—viz., a diminution in the quantity of blood contained, or else a complete emptying of important parts of the heart.

Reflections such as these, very naturally and for certainly sufficient reasons, lead to the formation of a definite plan of examination of the parts, which is in no way dependent upon personal caprice or considerations of convenience, but follows necessarily from the nature of the thing itself.

I do not here intend to offer any exhaustive exposition of the reasons why I adopt precisely that order of sequence of which the Regulations are the authoritative expression. I may venture to give, however, a few more explanations with regard to the order of sequence which is directed to be observed in examining the organs of the abdomen.

*a.* For cleanliness' sake I examine the intestines last. To deal with the contents of the intestines is, in itself, a very disagreeable matter. Even with the greatest care, one can scarcely avoid soiling one's self, the instruments and receptacles, the subject, and the table on which it lies. I will say nothing about the sense of smell, though it is a great puzzle to me how it is that some persons, when making autopsies, seem to have completely lost this sense. There is no possible disadvantage in examining, as a rule, the intestines last; for all the other parts can be conveniently examined, removed, and dealt with without the intestines being interfered with. If, however, any one attaches less importance to cleanliness,—if perhaps the physician is in a great hurry, and wishes especially to see the intestines examined,—there is no technical reason why this should not be done before meddling with the other viscera, for the intestines also can be removed without injuring the other parts. There is an exception in the case of the duodenum, inasmuch as the excretory ducts of the liver and pancreas open into it, and its removal is impossible without cutting through these ducts and even a portion of the pancreas.

*b.* The order of sequence which I adopt differs in one main point from that which was previously and formerly almost universally employed, inasmuch as I usually make the removal of the liver the last part but one of the examination. I am well aware that in so doing I depart essentially from the favourite custom. If the dissector places himself, as he usually does, on the right side of the body, having the head to his left, the liver is so immediately in front of his hand that it undoubtedly requires a sort of resignation to make up one's mind to leave it alone. But, irrespective of what I have already enlarged upon (that in the removal of the liver the large veins are injured, and, for the most part, the diaphragm as well), there is also this to be considered: that the hepato-duodenal ligament (the small omentum), and the tubes therein contained, especially the vena portæ and gall-duct, are injured more considerably and to greater disadvantage. I confess that these two last-mentioned structures are, in the great majority of cases, of no importance to the medical jurist, and if the order of sequence necessary for a clinical case were to be enjoined on him, it might certainly appear superfluous. On the other hand, however, it will be no disadvantage to him, and it will involve neither more time nor more trouble, whether he examines the liver first, or last but one; and even granting that the cases are but few in which the more correct method is requisite for the medico-legal investigation, this is quite a sufficient ground for requiring it to be universally adopted. For clinical investigation, the preservation of the hepato-duodenal ligament is of the greatest importance, because, if once divided, it is a mere chance if we succeed in replacing the parts in their natural position in such a way as to be able positively to elucidate their condition. It is here, however, that we have to look for thrombosis and obliterations of the vena portæ, and to estimate the condition, as regards perviousness, of the ductus communis choledochus, particularly of its intestinal portion, and also of the cystic and hepatic ducts. I may refer to a former paper of mine on these subjects. In my *Archives*, 1865, vol. xxxii. page 117, I have discussed the various conditions of the ductus communis choledochus and its intestinal portion, and have alluded to the importance of these for explaining the origination of jaundice; and in the *Transactions of the Würzburg Physico-Medical Society*, 1857, vol. vii. page 21, and in my "Gesammelten Abhandlungen," page 620, I have treated of obstructions of the vena portæ. The nature of the circumstances necessitates the following order of sequence in examining these parts. First we should open the duodenum, taking care to do so *in situ;* then determine its contents above and below the papilla biliaria ; then this papilla should be examined and its contents gently pressed out; then, by pressing on the gall-bladder, we should determine the presence or absence of obstacles to the flow of bile; and, lastly, the ductus communis choledochus should be slit up. Then the vena cava should be examined ; and, all this having been done, the liver should be removed. It is quite useless to pass a probe along the gall-duct, for our being able to introduce a probe into the orifice is no evidence whatever that the portio intestinalis was pervious during life.

*c.* The examination and opening of the stomach are closely connected with the above-mentioned operations. The simplest plan is to open the stomach at the same time as the duodenum, by continuing the incision; and this should, as a rule, be done *in situ.* Cases of poisoning, especially those which come under legal investigation, may require a different course. In other cases there is no danger in allowing the stomach to remain untouched until its turn comes. The spleen, the only organ closely connected with it, may, with moderate care, be so easily separated that there is no fear of causing damage. On the other hand, as is easily intelligible, the examination of the pancreas will follow that of the stomach and duodenum. The slight

importance of this organ, in a pathologico-anatomical point
of view, causes its examination to be of little consequence.

*d.* All the urinary organs should, as a matter of course,
be examined one after the other. We take them, therefore, in this sequence—the kidneys, the ureters, the urinary
bladder, and the urethra. At all events, their condition
will in this way be much more attentively examined than
if some other object of an entirely different nature be
allowed to intrude itself while the examination is going on.
It is also perfectly evident that the supra-renal capsules
and the generative organs must be examined in connection
with the urinary organs. They are immediately connected,
inasmuch as portions of the generative organs are portions
also of the urinary organs, so that for the sake of continuity of plan, and also for convenience in the removal of
the parts, the examination of the generative and of the
urinary organs should be performed at one and the same
time.

The order, therefore, which I adopt in examining the
abdominal organs is as follows:—

1. The omentum.

2. The spleen.

3. The left kidney, supra-renal capsule, and ureter.

4. The right kidney, supra-renal capsule, and ureter.

5. The bladder, prostate gland, vesiculæ seminales,
urethra.

6. (*a*) Testicles, spermatic cord, and penis.

   (*b*) Vagina, uterus, Fallopian tubes, ovaries, para-
   metria.

7. The rectum.

8. The duodenum, portio intestinalis of the ductus
communis choledochus.

9. Stomach.

10. Hepato-duodenal ligament, gall-ducts, vena portæ, gall-bladder, liver.

11. Pancreas, cœliac (semilunar) ganglia.

12. Mesentery, with its glands, vessels, etc.

13. Small and large intestine.

14. Retro-peritoneal lymphatic glands, receptaculum chyli, aorta, vena cava inferior.

However useful and convenient it may be to keep to such a regular plan, it is impracticable in a small number of cases, in which considerable changes have taken place in the relations and connections of the parts. Chronic adhesive peritonitis, whether occurring *per se*, in a simple, tuberculous, cancerous, or other form, or connected with tumours (*e.g.* ovarian), or with aneurism of the abdominal aorta, usually makes it impossible to dispense with the considerations peculiar to the case, and to adopt any general rule. Even in such cases it will be advisable to complete in the usual way the examination of those organs which can be easily reached, and thus to lessen gradually the special alterations which are requisite. But a departure from the rule is finally requisite, because it is, generally speaking, most convenient to remove together the remainder of the organs, and to examine them more particularly outside the body, in whatever way is the easiest.

So much with regard to the order of sequence in which the organs are to be examined, and the method of dissection.

The answer to the question, how to make incisions, belongs to quite another side of the subject. What I have to say in reference to this, is the primary result of simple experience, acquired by frequent practice and constant endeavours directed towards simplifying the operative portion of our task. But also, in addition to this, I endeavoured to account to myself for the reasons for my usual *modus operandi.* Thus became developed a systematic practice of the proper method of making incisions. The description, which I shall now give, is based upon grounds which were originally purely empirical, and which have only gradually become modified by additional theoretical considerations. In the first place, I assert emphatically that there must be an essential difference between the method of making incisions for pathological purposes and that which is adapted for the anatomical theatre or dissecting-room. In the ordinary way of making preparations, the young student is taught to hold his knife as he would a pen. The object is to make short fine cuts in order to expose muscles, nerves, and vessels, and to follow them out and show them clearly. Holding the knife in this way, the young student keeps his fingers in the position which became habitual to him, up to a certain point, when he was taught to write. The movements are confined almost entirely to the joints of the fingers—at any rate, to those of the hand. The arm itself is fixed generally in such a way that the elbow-joint is brought close to the trunk, and often to the thorax, unless, indeed, it rests on the crest of the ilium. In this way, short quick cuts may be made with great steadiness, the result of which is that neatness of appearance in a preparation which is appreciated in a moment by the sharp glance of the anatomical teacher. If such fine work be required for pathological anatomy—and this is the case pretty often,—not only is there no objection to this method, but it is absolutely requisite.

This, however, must not be considered to be the rule. An autopsy in which short incisions only are employed, is an unduly tedious affair, and both the pathological anatomist and the medical jurist have far less time at their disposal than is the case with the descriptive anatomist. On the other hand, numerous short incisions cause the larger organs to be too much divided, and partial cuts in no way assist the inspection, and appear to be adapted rather for kitchen purposes than for those of science. In examinations for pathological purposes, we save time and gain increased insight and clearness by making free incisions, and, when possible, such as involve the whole of the organ to be examined.

When this had become evident, I very soon perceived the necessity for holding the knife in a different manner. For all ordinary purposes of pathological dissection I now grasp the handle of the knife in the palm of my hand, so that when I stretch out my arm the blade appears as a direct prolongation. I fix then, relatively, if not absolutely, the joints of the fingers and hand, and make the cutting movements with the entire arm, so that the principal movements occur in the shoulder-joint, the secondary ones in the elbow-joint. In this way I am able to make long and useful incisions, and smooth ones as well, for I can utilise the whole force of the arm, and especially of the muscles about the shoulder ; and it is only on surfaces produced by such incisions as these that we are able to see anything really satisfactorily.

After I had got so far, I then perceived that in many roundabout ways I had reached the point which our predecessors in dissection, the butchers, had so long ago attained. I was not a little astonished when one day, not very long ago, I went into a slaughter-house and watched the men at their work. I then learned something else, which I have since brought into practice—viz., that the knife should be wider and longer than that commonly used.

A knife of such length and breadth, so well adapted for the butcher's purpose, is certainly inadmissible for ours, and it is only for the brain, and even then only in particularly important cases, that we require a very large flat-bladed knife which exceeds the dimensions even of those used in the slaughter-house. But a knife for making sections should always be very considerably larger than the ordinary knife used in making preparations. The latter is too short, both in the handle and in the blade, for making really large cuts. On the other hand, the blade is still too large for ordinary preparation purposes; for when held as a pen the point only of the knife is used—a portion measuring scarcely fifteen millimetres. The rest of the blade is so superfluous that the beginner in pathological technics, who comes to me to learn the art of dissecting, immediately takes the knife (which I place in his *hand*) between his *fingers*, and then moves them in a wriggling way forwards on the handle, until their points touch the steel of the blade. It is then naturally impossible to use the whole of the edge, for a large part of it is covered by the hand. As the dissector now finds himself confined to the point of his knife, and can use no other part of it, it is easy to understand that he very soon blunts it, and whereas a good pathological anatomist is perfectly able to dissect all the viscera of one subject, or even of two, with one knife, a pathological "layman," holding his knife as he would a pen, requires three or four knives for one autopsy.

The modified section-knife (*Secirmesser*) which I have introduced differs from the ordinary dissecting-knife (*Präparirmesser*) both in the blade and handle. Both these latter are not only longer, but stronger—that is, thicker and broader. The anterior part of the blade does not form an acute angle, but is rounded off; the very broad surface terminates with a considerable curve in the slightly projecting point. Thus, not only is the cutting edge still further lengthened, but, at the same time, the risk of pricking one's self or others, or of getting a prick from others, during the examination is considerably diminished. The number of dangerous wounds (and pricks are always more dangerous than cuts) has been very much diminished among us since we have adopted this useful kind of knife. As regards the back part of the knife, the blade is narrow and strong near its insertion, for this portion of it is generally not much used; the handle is flatter posteriorly, and much curved inwards from both edges, so that it may lie more conveniently in the hand. Such a knife is, in its original condition, before it has been ground down, twenty-three to twenty-four centimetres long, of which nine centimetres and a half belong to the blade.

This knife should really be used for making incisions with a traction movement. It should not be pressed or pushed into the parts, but should be drawn through them with comparative rapidity. When necessary, we may employ the whole force of the muscles of the shoulder in this movement, and much power can be thus exerted. But the greater the force employed, the quicker must be the movement, or else the parts are liable to become crushed. Nowhere can this be better proved than in the brain. Even a very sharp knife pressed into the brain crushes the parts to a certain extent, and the resulting cut surface is, at least in some measure, useless for examination; often, indeed, the appearance it presents leads directly to false conclusions.

An incision made by traction differs from one made by pressure primarily in this: that in the former every point of the edge glides over or through a certain spot in the organ; whereas in the latter the same point in the edge always presses upon the same spot of the organ. Whoever chooses to make incisions by pressure always, possibly involuntarily, places his forefinger on the back of the knife. He who makes incisions by traction places his forefinger on the surface of the handle, or he grasps the whole handle. At all events, it is a good practice, especially for beginners, to place the handle between the thumb and finger only, so that great pressure is impossible.

Where it is necessary really to exercise great pressure, we require another kind of knife—namely, one with a broader back, to which the forefinger or even the thumb may be conveniently applied. I have for this purpose made a further improvement on the ordinary cartilage-knife: the one which I use has a thicker and more bulging blade, and a much stronger handle. This latter is formed of two strong plates of wood or horn, one of these being applied to each side of a flat prolongation of the blade, reaching the

entire length of the handle. The back of such a knife
sixteen millimetres broad, is a convenient support when
pressure is required. The free end also of the handle is
flattened and broad, so that for certain purposes, such
as for separating the sterno-clavicular joint, it can be
placed vertically in the palm of the hand, and can be conveniently used for making punctures.

I therefore require for each examination three different
knives—an ordinary dissecting-knife (*Präparirmesser*), a
peculiar section-knife (*Secirmesser*), and a very strong
cartilage-knife. I use the last for all the coarser sort
of work—not merely for dividing cartilages, but also
for large incisions through skin, muscle, and joints. The
section-knife (*Secirmesser*) serves especially for dissecting
the large viscera; the dissecting-knife (*Präparirmesser*)
for the finer parts, vessels, nerves, etc. But inasmuch as
the examination of the large viscera is the primary object
of a pathological dissection, it is evident that the section-
knife in its present modified form is the principal instrument. In order to use it, the right arm must be allowed
to be quite free. The elbow must be raised quite away
from the trunk, so that the flexed forearm may be moved
freely, and in any direction backwards or forwards. It is,
then, easily practicable to divide the integuments of the
trunk by one single long incision from the chin to the
symphysis pubis. So, also, one incision is sufficient to
display the lung from apex to base in two halves. Perhaps this "dodge" (*Schwabenstreich*)—I use the word in
the sense of the worthy Frederick Barbarossa—may appear
to some improper and culpable. But I candidly own that
I am a fanatical admirer of a large incision. The freer
the incision—always supposing that it is an even one—the
larger will be the field of view, the more numerous will be
the points of comparison between normal and abnormal
parts, and the more exactly shall we be able to estimate the
extent of the pathological territories.

I maintain, indeed, that a free incision, even when

wrongly done, is, as a rule, to be preferred to a small, though accurate, one, and is almost always better than several or many small cuts. The large even cut is peculiarly the one for demonstration purposes. To make it, I look carefully at each separate organ, to find where I can get the largest surface on section. I therefore cut through a spleen from above downwards, over the middle of its outer (convex) surface, a kidney from without to within (from the external to the internal border), a liver from right to left in a horizontal direction; the testicle I cut into two nearly equal parts in a perpendicular direction from its free to its attached border, and snap the parts asunder. I divide each lobe of the lung by a perpendicular incision directed from above downwards, and from its thick border towards its inner (anterior, medial, sharp) one. Each hemisphere of the brain I divide by an incision beginning internally just over the corpus striatum, and directed somewhat obliquely outwards. Each hemisphere of the cerebellum I divide by an incision which commences in the fourth ventricle, in the direction of the crus cerebelli, and is carried obliquely outwards.

For many cases, and for several organs, one such cut is sufficient in order to show all that is essential. It very often happens that alterations in the liver, spleen, and kidneys are diffused so uniformly throughout the entire organ that one single cut affords us a sufficient insight into the internal structure of the parts. It is true that in other cases and in other organs—for example, always in the brain—we have to make a larger number of cuts in order to be sure that nothing has been overlooked. Indeed, in the case of the brain we can, properly speaking, never positively assert that it is quite normal, unless we divide it into quite microscopic portions according to the new method of Herr von Gudden. But as this is only practicable in exceptional cases, we must perforce be content with approximative methods. This epithet, however, cannot be applied to any method where sections five millimetres thick are

made of important parts.  In the interior of such a section
there is always plenty of room for foci of morbid material
sufficient to produce paralysis or convulsions.  The less
we find, the greater the number of sections we ought to
make.

But whether we make few or many incisions, it seems
expedient in every case not to carry them so far as completely to separate the portions of the organ.  Even if we
only make one single cut, it is always useful to leave in one
spot so much of the parts connected as to be able easily to
restore the external form of the organ by merely placing
the parts together and adjusting them.  Many an idea
with reference to external appearances has occurred only
after the inspection of internal changes has directed our
attention to certain conditions; and it is much easier to
restore the form and general appearance of an organ when
the natural continuity of the parts has been to some extent
preserved, than when their connexions have been completely
severed.

In those instances in which the necessity of the case
demands that the incisions should be greatly multiplied—
as, for example, in the brain and spinal cord—it would be
utterly impossible to form any further opinion as to the
extent of certain changes, or even as to their exact locality,
or their relation to the vessels, etc., if the parts have been
completely divided.  It often happens here that, only at a
late stage of the examination, changes become prominent,
which render it desirable to re-examine, once or more
frequently, all the cut parts in their natural order of
sequence, to convince ourselves that nothing has been overlooked in our first examination.  Very simple precautions
are required to rearrange the parts of an organ thus dissected: it resembles a book, the leaves of which can be
opened here and there, or even entirely separated, and
then again closed.  But the object in having a book bound
is to secure to every leaf a definite place, where it can be
found in a moment without much trouble.

The question now arises as to the place to be selected for the "binding of the book." A close consideration of the relations of each separate organ enables us to answer this question with facility. The continuity must be in all cases preserved exactly where the connection between the organ and adjoining parts is the most important.

In all the large glandular organs, as in those which resemble glands (the spleen and lungs), the incision should be made from the outside, and we should take care of the spots where the vessels enter and leave, where the excretory ducts make their exit, and where the nerves reach the organ. These spots are called the hilus, porta, or root —the name varying with the organ. If, after the incision has been made, the organ is found to exhibit any important alteration, which may possibly be due to a primary vascular lesion, or be the result of some slow morbid process in the excretory ducts, we can, if the hilus has been preserved, either probe, dissect, inject, or use the blow-pipe from the more distant portions of the vessels or canals. If one of these methods is unsuccessful, another of them will be practicable.

The circumstances are different in the case of the brain and spinal cord. Here the only "binding" is the pia mater which supports the vessels. Transverse incisions must therefore be made on the spinal cord, leaving the pia mater attached on the anterior or posterior surface, according as the incision has been made from the one or the other aspect. In the brain the incisions should always be directed through the hemispheres from within to without; so that, notwithstanding the number of cuts which it may be necessary to make in the internal parts, it may always be practicable, at the close of the examination, to put the brain together again. My general rule is that each successive incision should be made across the middle of the existing cut surface, and that each new half should be again and again divided.

This procedure is naturally not practicable in the large

ganglia. The optic thalamus and corpus striatum cannot
be so divided that the pia mâter may serve as a " binding "
to them. The reticulated membrane which reaches them,
the velum interpositum with its choroid plexus, comes in
contact with only a small streak, the so-called stria, or
lamina cornea, and must be stripped off before the dissection of the large ganglia is commenced. These latter I
divide by fan-shaped radial incisions, whose common start-
ing-point is the peduncle of the cerebrum. However great
the number of these incisions may be—and it is necessary
here to make numerous cuts,—the relationship of the parts
may always be closely preserved in consequence of the
connection between each separate portion and the peduncle
of the cerebrum.

Before I go on with my description, this appears to me
to be the place to say a few more words with reference to
the examination of the cerebral ventricles, in order to con-
clude in some degree my account of the method of dissecting the brain. My opinion is that the examination of the
brain, after the membranes have been finished, should
commence with the opening of the ventricles, since, apart
from any tearing or squeezing caused by manipulation,
the very weight of the organ increases the liability to
laceration as time goes on, and the consequent risk of the
escape of the fluids. The first incision, therefore, which I
generally make into the brain, is carried directly into a
lateral ventricle.

This incision, however, is not to be made in the way very
common, even now, in examining the lateral ventricles for
descriptive anatomy. The custom is, first to expose the
so-called centrum semi-ovale of Vieussens, and then to
create cerebral ventricles—perhaps by digging, almost in
mining fashion, with the handle of the scalpel. We ought
rather to bear in mind that between the middle portions
(cellæ mediæ) of the lateral ventricles there is only the very
thin septum lucidum to form a partition-wall, and that
it is exactly under the raphe of the corpus callosum. If we

therefore make a lateral incision, at a distance of one millimetre from this raphe, perpendicularly into the corpus callosum, we come directly into a cella media at a depth of two to three millimetres. This incision, which forms a right angle with the plane of the centrum semi-ovale, should be the first one made in the brain, unless a deviation is rendered necessary by any peculiar circumstances.

But this incision is naturally not sufficient to open the ventricle completely. In order to open the anterior and posterior cornua, or, at least, to demonstrate their condition (for the posterior cornua are more frequently completely or partially obliterated than open), it is necessary to make particular incisions anteriorly and posteriorly. These should not be made vertically, but horizontally, the anterior one higher, the posterior one deeper, in the anterior and posterior lobes of the brain. Then only we obtain a view of the lateral ventricles in their whole extent, for the entrance, at least, to the descending cornu is also exposed by the incision towards the posterior cornu.

Having determined the contents of the lateral ventricles, the state of their walls and venous plexus, and the condition of the septum, the latter is taken hold of with the left hand close behind the foramen of Monro, the knife is pushed in front of the fingers through this aperture, and the corpus callosum cut through obliquely, upwards and forwards, and then all these parts (corpus callosum, septum lucidum, and fornix) are carefully detached from the velum interpositum and its choroid plexus. After these two latter have been exposed, we have to examine the state of their vessels and tissue. Then the handle of the scalpel is passed from the front, under the velum, which is thus detached from the pineal body and corpora quadrigemina, the state of these parts is determined, and the third ventricle now exposed. Lastly, with a long perpendicular incision, we divide the corpora quadrigemina and the cerebellum as far as the aqueduct of Sylvius and the fourth ventricle.

In the case of the brain, the pathologico-anatomical examination has to take a course peculiar to itself, and one which differs in many respects from that adopted in descriptive anatomy; and the above statement may suffice to demonstrate the most convenient and rapid method of dissecting with a view to a certain object. It at the same time most clearly shows that here also a free incision is to be preferred to any other mode of division, and, as I again repeat, the incision should be made by traction. It is of the greatest consequence that the incisions should be even and smooth in an organ like the brain, where the separate portions are of so great importance, and where one part is distinguished from another by peculiarity of function. How could we possibly demonstrate small foci of softening or induration upon an uneven, crushed, or torn surface? And these two are exactly those changes most frequently occurring in the brain. Therefore I say to my students, "Smooth, though wrong, incisions rather than correct and uneven ones!" It is true that with an incision made in a wrong direction we can scarcely tell what we are about, but an incision badly made is entirely worthless.

On account of the importance of the subject, I shall now describe in detail the examination of a second organ, in order to explain the peculiarity of my method and the reasons for adopting it.

What I refer to is the dissection of the heart; and although the general principles which I have laid down apply also to this organ, yet the details to be taken into account are so multifarious that numerous modifications of the general rules become requisite.

After we have opened the pericardium and determined its condition, and also ascertained the external appearance and the position of the heart, its size, shape, colour, consistence, the amount of blood contained in the superficial vessels, the amount of fat in the sub-pericardial tissue, etc., we have then to open the heart,—and we should do this *in situ*. In making this first opening, we have in view two objects : the determination of the quantity of blood in the separate cavities, and the examination of the capacity of the auriculo-ventricular orifices. Such an examination is, of course, indispensably necessary. The determination of the quantity and quality of the blood contained in the different parts of the heart is of decisive importance for ascertaining the kind of death. It is in the highest degree probable, even if not absolutely certain, that two of the most important kinds of death—that from asphyxia (*Erstickungstod*), and that from paralysis of the heart (*Herzschlag, Apoplexia cordis*)—occur in consequence of the over-filling, in the first case, of the right ventricle, in the second, of the left. We must, however, for clinical, and partly for forensic purposes, examine the capacity of the auriculo-ventricular orifices, especially of the one on the left side.

Another question which may be raised with reference to the auriculo-ventricular orifices can, unfortunately, only in certain cases be answered from sufficient evidence. I refer to the question with regard to their capacity for closing (*continentia*, less accurately though more frequently described as *sufficientia*). In an ordinary post-mortem examination no method can be adopted whereby the capacity for closing of the auriculo-ventricular valves can be thoroughly tested. We must content ourselves with supplying this deficiency by a minute examination of the valvular parts; and I will here remark that for this purpose it is absolutely requisite to preserve in their integrity all the parts belonging to the auriculo-ventricular valves, therefore also the chordæ tendineæ and the musculi papillares.

A consideration of the two objects to be kept in view in making the first opening in the heart teaches us that on both sides the base of the organ must be preserved,—for to the base on the right side the slips of the tricuspid valve are attached ; on the left side those of the mitral ; and, therefore, if we cut through the base, we injure at least one of the slips of these valves on each side. In addition to which it would be quite impossible to estimate the quantity of blood contained in each side, therefore also in each auricle and each ventricle, unless we open each of them separately. It therefore follows that for the first portion of the examination of the heart four separate incisions are required.[*]

There can scarcely be any dispute as to the position and direction of these incisions. The mechanism of the heart allows no great choice with regard to the spots to be selected. Variations are possible only within certain limits. My method of dissecting the heart may be described under the following heads :—

1. The right border of the heart is the natural and recognised place of incision for examining the right ventricle. The incision must here begin close to the base, and must be carried at once deeply and forcibly into the interior of the ventricle; towards the apex the knife must be brought out without going too far down, for otherwise there is considerable risk of cutting the septum.

2. This incision is at the same time the guide for the three others; and the place for the incision for each separate portion of the heart is to be found in a plane taking the direction of the first incision.

3. The incision for the right auricle commences half-way between the places of entrance of the venæ cavæ, and ends just in front of the base.

4. The incision for the left auricle commences at the left superior pulmonary vein, and ends in like manner just in front of the base, which is usually indicated by the very prominent coronary vein. We should carefully avoid injuring the coronary vessels.

5. The incision through the left ventricle begins just

* See Pl. 1.

Fig.1.

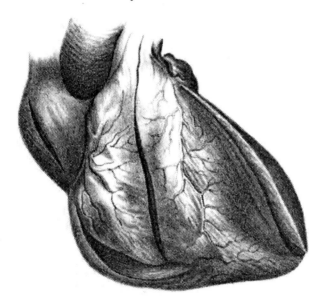

behind the base, and ends just short of the apex. It must be carried deeply and forcibly through the wall of the heart.

6. To bring the heart into the right position for the dissection, when the incisions for the right side are to be made, I extend firmly the forefinger of the left hand, and push it under the heart, and keep it against the base, so that the ventricular portion hangs down over the forefinger, which is as a fulcrum to it (*Hypomochlion*). Then I turn the heart on its axis towards the left until the right border presents anteriorly, and I press the thumb of the left hand just behind this border at the base. When the heart is thus fixed, I make, one after the other, both the incisions for the right side.

7. In dealing with the left side, I seize the apex of the heart, draw it upwards and to the left, and place the heart in the left hand in such a way that my fingers can encircle it. Then, with gentle pressure, I make the posterior wall to bulge out a little, and withdraw itself from the septum. Then I make in like manner, one after the other, the incisions for the left side.

So much for the method to be adopted in making the incisions. I have now described in a connected way all that is necessary; but in practice the determination of the quantity of blood contained in the chambers, and of the size of the auriculo-ventricular orifices, intervenes during these operations. That is to say, after making the incisions in the right side of the heart, I first remove the blood from the right auricle, and determine its quantity and quality; then I insert two fingers of the left hand (the index and middle fingers) from the auricle through the tricuspid opening into the ventricle, and endeavour to open this latter cavity. Then I remove the blood from the right ventricle, and determine it as before. I then do the same on the left side.

With reference to the examination of the auriculo-ventricular orifices, I may again remark that in this first stage nothing but their size should be ascertained. The examiner must therefore not be tempted to introduce his finger at present for the purpose of feeling whether, and to what extent, the valves are altered. This can be done later on, when the parts can not only be felt and handled, but are also fully exposed to view. Every attempt now made to ascertain, by feeling or rubbing, the condition of the borders of the valves is calculated to produce alterations or to remove any that may be present: any adherent coagula, for example, may be easily broken up or altogether detached. When the two fingers have been introduced, and the size of the orifice determined, they must be withdrawn as gently as possible. I shall here remark that each individual examiner must find out for himself by experience how far his fingers are a measure of the normal size of the orifices. For thin fingers, as in my own case, we may assume that the tricuspid orifice permits the introduction not merely of the index and middle fingers in apposition, but that we may separate the two fingers to such a distance from each other as to be able to introduce between them from the ventricle a third finger, e.g., the index finger of the right hand. With large and thick fingers this is not practicable. We have, moreover, on the left side to take into consideration the contracted condition of the heart. If the left ventricle is strongly contracted, the contraction will extend to the base of the heart, which is equivalent to the base of the orifice. We must then gently press the walls asunder, in order to overcome the contraction and the rigor mortis which is also very often present; this can be done without difficulty. It is only after the state of contraction has been overcome that we are able to form an opinion as to the actual size of the orifice.

These investigations terminate the first act in the examination of the heart. The removal of the heart is the first step of the second act. To do this we seize the organ by introducing the index-finger of the left hand into the left ventricle, and the thumb into the right, through the already existing incisions. We then raise up the apex, and with it the whole of the heart, and then, with three or four long, free, horizontal incisions, we divide the venæ cavæ and the pulmonary veins, the pulmonary artery and the aorta, all together, taking care that the incisions are not too close to the heart. When the heart has been removed, we first examine the cut openings of the aorta and pulmonary artery, determine the size of these vessels and the thickness of their walls, and remove from them any existing coagula.

Then we investigate the capacity for closure of the arterial orifices by pouring water into the aorta and pulmonary artery. Before we do this, we must be always certain that all coagula have been removed, not only from the vessels, but also from the orifices and the ventricles. For it is clear that coagula in any of these parts may so occlude an insufficient orifice as to give the impression of one that is sufficient. When the water is poured in, the heart must be held freely suspended in the air, for, if it is supported, a portion of the wall of the heart may be brought in contact with, and may stop up, the orifice we are examining. We must also avoid taking the heart in the hand and encircling it with the fingers, for we should in that way compress it, and prevent the escape of water through the orifice. The proper plan is to fix the heart by applying the points of the fingers of both hands either to the vessels to be examined, or externally near the base of the valves, in such a way that the plane of the orifice is exactly horizontal, and not drawn to any side. For in an oblique position of the orifice the weight on the separate portions of the valve becomes unequal, and fluid may escape through a valve which would otherwise close ; and if the parts be dragged or stretched in a lateral direction, so that the circular lumen of the vessel is made to assume a crescentic form, the conditions of normal closure which involve the coming together of corresponding parts of the valve no longer exist. We must, therefore, always use both hands in order to suspend the heart properly, and the water must be poured in by a second person.

The best way to suspend the heart, when we are examining the aortic orifice, is to find a series of points where the tips of the fingers can be closely applied round it, and these are to be found on the right and left auricles and pulmonary artery. To apply one's fingers simply to the edges of the opening in the aorta is always somewhat hazardous, for there is then only room to hold the vessel in two places; and if we limit ourselves to these, we are always apt to stretch the parts unequally. Moreover, in every case the aorta should be again divided at a distance of four or five centimetres above the orifice, by an incision parallel to the plane of the aperture. We are then able, while the water is being poured in, to observe the condition of the separate portions of the valve, and to ascertain positively the spots where the water escapes. I make, in conclusion, one remark—that sometimes the water sinks, and finally quite disappears, without passing away through the orifice. In this case it usually escapes through the coronary arteries, which are often divided when the left side of the heart is first opened. Particular attention must therefore be paid to this point.

In the pulmonary artery the majority of these difficulties do not exist; we can therefore, without any further preparation, almost always contrive to suspend the heart for the purpose of testing the pulmonary orifice by fixing between the fingers the edges of the opening into the vessel.

We now come to the third part of the examination of the heart: the opening of both the ventricles.

For this purpose, the best plan is to place the heart exactly in the position which it occupied in the body, upon a board or table, and then to make the necessary incisions.

Fig. 2.

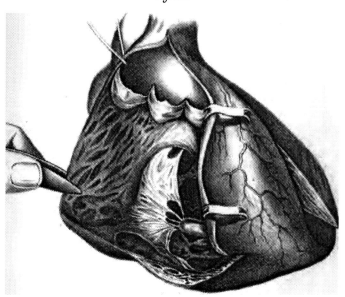

This has the advantage of exposing to view the directions the incisions are to take. The interior of the heart ought by means of the following incisions, to be made so far accessible to eye and finger that the parts remaining to be examined can be conveniently reached. Among these we must mention, in the first place, the auriculo-ventricular valves with their chordæ tendineæ and musculi papillares. Afterwards come the cavities themselves, their endocardial investment, the arterial valves, the septum between the ventricles and that between the auricles, and the muscular substance itself. The auriculo-ventricular valves are here first mentioned, not on account of their peculiar importance, but because the want, previously alluded to, of a proper closure test for them makes it requisite to subject them to a much more minute examination, and to preserve them in their integrity until this has been done. With regard to the arterial valves, which have meanwhile been thoroughly tested and examined with reference to their capacity for closing, the same kind of care is no longer necessary. These considerations determine the directions of the incisions requisite for the complete opening of the ventricles.

(a.) The incision for the right ventricle * is in a straight line prolonged from the pulmonary artery, and near the base of the heart. The best instrument for this purpose is a long pair of scissors, such as those used for examining the intestines. One blade of the scissors is inserted into the previous incision made in the right border, and carried in a direction towards the pulmonary artery. There is just one thing to bear in mind, and that is, that in this direction we come upon the anterior papillary muscle of the tricuspid valve with its chordæ tendineæ; and this must be carefully preserved. If this or its chordæ tendineæ be cut through, we shall not be able subsequently to demonstrate perfectly the arrangement of the valves of the tricuspid opening. The blade of the scissors must be introduced in front of this papillary muscle, and the incision through

* See Pl. 2

the anterior wall of the ventricle and of the pulmonary artery must, as described, be carried close to the base.

(b.) The incision for the left ventricle,* which should also be made with a long pair of scissors, is in a straight line prolonged from the ascending aorta, and close to the septum ventriculorum. It commences at the apex of the heart, and divides the anterior wall of the ventricle and of the aorta. The part which here requires the greatest care and attention is the base of the mitral valve; and the explanation of this is as follows:—If we cut directly upwards from the apex of the heart to the aortic orifice, keeping too close to the septum, the incision will cross the pulmonary orifice, and, by simply continuing the same, we shall cut through the valves of the pulmonary artery. This can be avoided by drawing the pulmonary artery to the right when making the incision, and by continuing this to the left, close to and behind the artery. But we must not go too far towards the left; there is a Charybdis here to be . avoided. The right border of the base of the mitral valve is inserted quite close to this spot, and this valve, as is well known, is connected immediately with the left border of the aortic orifice. If the incision goes only a few millimetres too much to the left, we shall cut off that portion of the mitral valve which forms the above-named junction; and then, if we attempt to put together the divided portions of the heart, we shall find an aperture in the mitral valve. Externally, this spot corresponds exactly with the right border of the base of the left auricle. This should be our guide. The incision must therefore be carried through midway between the pulmonary orifice and the left auricle.

The principal part of the examination is now finished. The auricles can, however, be still further opened by cutting through their wall with the scissors, between the openings of the venæ cavæ on the right, and of the pulmonary veins on the left side. Further incisions can also

* See Pl. 3.

Fig 3.

be made into the muscular substance; for example, some very important ones running parallel to the surface from those last made in the ventricles, and which divide the wall of the heart into an inner and an outer half. The coronary arteries can also be further slit up, the incisions hitherto made having, upon the whole, but little interfered with these vessels. In exceptional and peculiar cases, such steps as these may have to be taken; but, as a general rule, the examination is completed in the three acts which have been detailed, and which are also indispensable. The heart cannot possibly be regularly examined unless these three acts are properly performed.

One might suppose, after reading the long description which I have just given, that it would take a long time for all this to be carried out. The reader's idea might be similar to that of an unfortunate district physician, who, after studying the new Regulations, came to the conclusion that to make an autopsy in the prescribed manner would require at least two days. The one notion is as erroneous as the other. Ten minutes are sufficient to examine the heart in the way I have described, and an autopsy can be performed according to the new Regulations in three hours, and even in two where there are but few complications.

In order to be able to judge for myself as to the requirements of the Regulations, I have taken a few suitable cases, and made the post-mortem examinations in the prescribed form. I give, by way of a supplement, the notes of these examinations as instances, and also, in a certain sense, as models. I do not mean that they should (like Caspar's autopsies) serve as examples of diction and technics, and should relieve those who make examinations from describing and specifying in their own way what they find before them; but what I intend is that they should show what a report is like when the Regulations have been carried out. A certain amount of freedom has been used in dictating these notes, and a very critical eye may possibly discover a few places where the Regulations have not been complied with, and some strictures may be made thereupon. But these, I hope, are such subordinate points that there will be at least no necessity for any " revision notes " (*Revisionsbemerkungen*) in the sense in which this word is used by the Committee of Sciences.

The cases which I have selected are also of some interest in other respects, and I shall take the liberty of interpolating a few critical remarks.

## CASE I.

A man unknown. Dead when brought in ; face covered with blood ; left side of face, particularly about the ear, of a bluish-red colour. Death from suffocation caused by pulmonary hæmorrhage and œdema.

Length of time occupied in the examination, two hours and five minutes. November, 1875.

### A. *External Examination.*

1. The body is that of a man apparently from forty to fifty years of age ; height 1·75 metre (68·89 inches) ; very strongly built ; adipose tissue slight in quantity ; muscles greatly developed,—those of the arm and thigh less so in proportion than those of the forearm and leg.

2. Body generally pale in colour ; abdomen slightly green ; flanks posteriorly, scrotum and glans of a uniform bluish-red ; dorsum the same, and pale only where exposed to pressure ; on pressing with the finger this bluish-red colour can be made to disappear, not easily, though tolerably completely. On an incision being made, only distended vessels are visible in the skin and subcutaneous tissues, from which fluid blood escapes.

3. The body being turned over for the purpose of this examination, a thin sanguineous fluid escapes from the nose and mouth.

4. The face, particularly the left side as far as the ear, and the beard are much soiled with dried blood, the largest quantity being on the nostrils and lips. A brownish-red, dry, powdery substance, on the left side converted into larger coherent crusts of dried blood, covers the neck and upper part of the chest.

5. Hair of head abundant, curly, light brown in colour; numerous scattered grey hairs. The beard full, especially about the chin; whiskers strongly developed, colour more reddish-brown; eyebrows thick and, like the eyelashes, of a dark greyish-brown colour; pupil pale greyish-blue; face large; forehead prominent; nose large and straight; high cheek-bones; front teeth perfect; molar teeth more or less carious and defective; no traces of recent injury; lips pale and thin.

6. The body presents no other particular characteristics, only that the prepuce is unusually short, and covers no more than the edge of the glans; there is, however, no cicatrix of any kind to be seen.

7. The hands large; the nails long and bluish, the projecting edges filled up with thick black dirt, traces of which are seen also in the palms of the hands.

8. There is some amount of mobility in the principal joints of the extremities, but there are signs of rigor mortis in all the smaller articulations.

9. The eyelids are only partially closed; the cornea transparent, and comparatively tense.

10. No foreign body about the nostrils, with the exception of the blood already mentioned.

11. The lips, as well as the teeth, are slightly parted; the tongue is behind the teeth, and, like the palate, covered with fluid blood.

12. External parts of ears unusually large; the left ear of a dark brown-red colour. On an incision being made, blood flows everywhere copiously from the divided vessels,

but there is no sign of extravasated blood in the tissue; auditory meatus empty.

13. Neck not very easily movable; no change perceptible.

14. Chest full; abdomen slightly distended.

15. Cutis anserina slightly marked on the extremities, especially on the lower ones; the legs above the ankles rather large, pitting on pressure; the tissues on section found to be infiltrated with fluid. Just above the ankles there is a loose knotted piece of cord, twisted round each of them; corresponding to this there is a transverse indentation on the inner and anterior aspects. This, when cut into, exhibits no extravasation of blood.

16. The parts about the anus much soiled with brown excrement; the anus closed.

17. In conclusion, there is no perceptible mark of external injuries.

B. *Internal Examination.*—I. *The Cranial Cavities.*

18. The soft parts covering the skull are divided, as directed, by an incision carried transversely over the head, and reflected back. All these parts are then seen to be somewhat red in colour, the alteration being more marked posteriorly than in front—the redness, however, not being sufficiently distinct on any one spot for it to indicate extravasation; on the other hand, thick blood exudes everywhere from the divided vessels, and the soft parts appear to be uniformly infiltrated with reddish serum.

19. The skull-cap, very broad and much arched, exhibits posteriorly a similar reddish infiltration of its tissue, especially at the sutures, which are deeply indented, and furnished in various places with ossa triquetra. The colour of the remaining portions of the skull-cap is a dirty yellowish-grey, somewhat more whitish in isolated spots.

20. The skull-cap is sawn through with difficulty, and, when divided, cannot be taken off from the tough dura mater. The latter is therefore immediately cut through. On attempting to detach the bone and dura mater, the brain also follows, and this latter has to be removed by separating methodically its connections in the base of the skull.

21. The brain being removed, there is no appearance of serum nor of any other effusion on the basis cranii. The large sinuses in that situation contain only a moderate amount of fluid blood.

22. There is some difficulty in separating the tough dura mater from the base of the skull and the posterior portions. There is no sign of any kind of injury to the bones of the base.

23. There is no change, also, on the base of the brain itself. The great arteries are large, but flat and empty. The pia mater everywhere fine and soft, and its veins only filled with blood near their origin.

24. After the removal of the brain from the roof of the skull, the inner surface of the dura mater is found to be everywhere of a pale colour. There is no deposit connected with it; it is somewhat thick and tendinous; the longitudinal sinus large, but filled throughout with fluid blood.

25. The dura mater is then removed from the roof of the skull. Its external surface is also pale; the blood-vessels very prominent, but empty.

26. Neither fissure nor injury of any kind visible in the roof of the skull; diploë scanty in amount. The bones, on an average, are from five to six millimetres thick. Fine, red, very vascular, soft growths on the inner surface of the frontal bone in the middle line.

27. The surface of the brain well formed; the pia mater delicate throughout; the veins filled with blood, tumid

even to roundness on the left side, somewhat less so upon the right.

28. On cutting into them, the lateral ventricles are found to contain a small, inappreciable quantity of clear fluid. Cavities of normal size; posterior cornua obliterated. Septum soft, and easily torn; choroid plexus and vessels of the velum of a dark red colour, owing to great distension. The vessels separable only with difficulty from the corpora quadrigemina.

29. On cutting into the hemispheres of the brain the tissue is found to be moist and glistening; the white substance exhibits numerous bloody points, from which drops of blood exude on pressure; these drops can be washed away with water. The grey substance of the cortex pale reddish; that of the corpus striatum and of the thalamus similar in appearance, and also moist. No other change. Consistence of the brain good.

30. Corpora quadrigemina pale. Pineal gland small and red.

31. The fourth ventricle empty; its surface pale and soft, its choroid plexuses reddened.

32. The cortex of the cerebellum reddened throughout, though the vessels are not perceptible; the medullary substance, on the contrary, traversed by congested venous branches. Consistence good; moisture moderate in quantity. No change.

33. At the base of the brain, all the lobes cut through by numerous parallel transverse incisions; no alteration of any kind apparent. The grey substance slightly reddened throughout.

34. The grey substance of the pons Varolii and the cerebral peduncles of a reddish colour; the white substance traversed by numerous congested veins. Consistence good.

35. The medulla oblongata pale; the grey matter of the rhomboid fossa somewhat more reddened.

## II. *Thorax and Abdomen.*

. 36. A long incision is made from the chin to the pubic symphysis as directed, the integuments divided, and the cavity of the abdomen laid open. Adipose tissue slightly developed; muscles somewhat pale.

37. No foreign body in the abdominal cavity. Position of the parts normal. Cæcum, transverse colon, and the ascending portion of the large intestine are much distended; also a portion of the small intestine—in part with gas, and in part apparently with fluid. All these parts are pale in colour; the omentum only presents a few distended veins.

38. The arch of the diaphragm on each side is between the fourth and fifth ribs.

### (a.) *The Thorax.*

39. After removal of the sternum the lungs come into view, somewhat distended, particularly the left one; position of the parts normal in other respects. The pericardium to a great extent covered by the lungs.

40. On the left side several very firm adhesions between the surface of the lung and the wall of the thorax. A tablespoonful of thin reddish fluid in the most posterior part of the pleural cavity.

41. On the right side the adhesions to the upper lobe are somewhat more extensive, but equally firm, and traversed by vessels. A smaller amount of fluid than on the left side. Internally, near the pericardium, the adhesions are still more extensive.

42. The pericardium contains a tablespoonful of a slightly reddish but clear fluid.

43. The heart about the size of the man's fist, its right surface flattened, a slight amount of tendinous deposit (*Sehnenflecke*, maculæ albidæ), the right ventricle mode-

E.

rately covered with fat, pale, and only the coronary veins somewhat distended with blood. The right auricle contains particularly fluid blood, mixed with a very small quantity of soft, friable, buffy clot. The quantity of blood collected from the right side of the heart and the large veins amounts to 150 cubic centimetres. The right ventricle contains fluid blood only, inappreciable in quantity. The left auricle contains fluid blood and a small quantity of thick blood. The left ventricle quite empty. The blood everywhere equally dark. The aorta three centimetres in diameter, its walls thick, inner coat especially thickened. The pulmonary artery about the same size, but with thin walls. The valves at the mouths of both vessels close. On section, right ventricle found to be dilated, left ventricle large. Muscular tissue somewhat dark; a little paler on the right side. Valves without alteration, but of a deep red colour.

44. The large veins of the neck moderately distended with fluid blood; arteries empty. The large nerves apparently unaltered.

45. The cavity of the mouth opened, as directed, from beneath; the tongue drawn away, and the upper part of the throat exposed. All these parts covered with a layer of bloody mucus, which, however, can be easily rubbed off; after its removal the mucous membrane appears slightly reddened, but otherwise unchanged. Lingual follicles large, whitish. Tonsils slightly swollen.

46. A considerable quantity of bloody froth with large bubbles in the larynx and upper portion of the air-tubes. This removed, the mucous membrane appears only slightly reddened; on the posterior aspect of the tubes the vessels of the mucous membrane distended with blood, but no other change.

47. The remaining thoracic viscera, with the lungs, are now removed, together with the costal pleura.

48. Lower portion of the œsophagus is covered with reddish fluid, which can be easily taken off. After its removal, no alteration visible in the subjacent mucous membrane.

49. There is slight dilatation, and thickening of the internal coat, of the thoracic portion of the aorta, but no breach of surface. The same may be said of the large branches of the artery going to the neck.

50. The upper part of the air-tubes, as well as their large ramifications, are filled with frothy and bloody matter.

51. The lungs seem large, very concave on their diaphragmatic surface, studded over, especially on the right side, with smooth projections of their tissue greatly dilated (emphysematous). The lungs, in general, are grey in colour, pale anteriorly, reddened posteriorly. Numerous furrows, due to absorption on the anterior surface. These latter places feel harder to the touch; the rest of the tissue is soft, but only slightly crepitant.

52. On section, in the apex of the right lung is found a ramified cavity of irregular shape, about six centimetres and a half in diameter, consisting of two compartments, separated by a thin septum, and each of them four centimetres and a half in horizontal diameter. Each contains a bloody, slightly frothy liquid, which can be easily removed by water. The walls of both these cavities are irregular and rough, and, on water being poured upon them, they are seen to be covered with adhesions, which readily float. Many large eroded vessels, some of them lying free like rafters, are found in these cavities, into which branches of the air-tubes may be directly traced. In other parts of the lung there are single smaller cavities with smoother walls, and also separate circumscribed spots, externally hard to the touch, some of which appear on section dense, dull, greyish-red, and finely granular; others dry, greyish-white, and caseous. The rest of the

pulmonary tissue is full of frothy, whitish fluid, which can be easily pressed out.

53. On the left side, below the apex, more towards the centre of the upper lobe, there are several similar cavities, varying in size from that of a walnut to a hen's egg, containing also fluid, slightly frothy blood, and connected with the air-passages. The wall of these cavities is irregular and ragged; the remains of the large vessels appear as whitish projections. There is a similar cavity about as large as a walnut in the upper part of the lower lobe. Throughout the remainder of the lung there are numerous nodules of varying size—some as large as peas; a few with cavities in their interior; others solid and caseous; others, again, solid and dark grey.

### b. The Abdomen.

54. Spleen closely adherent to the diaphragm and omentum; fourteen centimetres long, nine centimetres broad, three centimetres and a half thick; externally, grey steel-coloured. On section, dark brown-red; pulp abundant with numerous dark red spots; follicles slightly enlarged.

55. Left kidney thirteen centimetres long, six centimetres and a half broad, three centimetres and a half thick. Capsule slightly dull, thin. Surface of the kidney smooth, brownish-red, bright; consistence firm. On section, the medullary and cortical substance very red, not dull; no other change. Malpighian corpuscles bloodless. Suprarenal capsule with a small amount of cortical and medullary substance; the tissue connecting it with the kidney firm and well supplied with blood.

56. On separating the parts surrounding the right kidney a fibrous adhesion between the large intestine and the under surface of the right lobe of the liver brought into view.

57. Right kidney of same size as left, and resembling it in other particulars. Supra-renal capsule in a similar condition.

58. Bladder contracted, and containing only a few drops of whitish urine. No change in mucous membrane.

59. Left testicle somewhat mis-shapen in consequence of fibrous adhesions on its surface. An offset from the right one at the upper part of the epididymis.

60. The stomach distended, and containing a large quantity (about 200 cubic centimetres) of thick, clotted, bloody fluid, mingled to some extent with large air-bubbles.

61. Fluid of a similar kind in the commencement of the duodenum, but extending only as far as the opening of the gall-duct. After this the contents are of a pale yellowish colour. Opening of gall-duct normal.

62. The mucous membrane of the stomach tinged throughout with blood, but without any lesion ; only the large veins distended with blood.

63. In the upper part of the intestine a large amount of a grey fluid resembling gruel, slightly coloured with bile. This becomes thinner and more scanty in the upper part of the jejunum. The ileum contains a very large quantity of fluid of a brownish colour. This part of the bowel is so soft that it tears when cut into with the scissors. The lowest part of the ileum contains a quantity of very fluid fæces. The large intestine from the ileo-cæcal valve full of thick pulpy fæces. The mucous membrane throughout the ileum thin and pale ; the glands slightly tumid. In the jejunum the mucous membrane is thicker. Here and there a single gland appears tumid, but in other respects normal. In the upper part of the jejunum the mucous membrane has a whitish appearance.

64. The liver (twenty-eight centimetres broad, twenty-three centimetres from front to back, and eight centimetres

thick) is firm to the touch, its surface of a pale brownish colour, somewhat firm under the knife; breaks with difficulty, and appears on section uniformly red. The lobules are large, and their colour uniform.

65. The inferior vena cava contains fluid blood.

This case is a remarkable instance of ulcerous consumption of the lung, occurring in a man in other respects vigorously developed, and in whom the disease, though obviously of long standing, had confined itself to the lungs. Owing to the advanced stage of the disease, it cannot be ascertained whether the morbid process primarily originated in bronchiectasis or caseous pneumonia; at any rate, caseous pneumonia finally supervened. It is a matter of great interest that, notwithstanding the amount of hæmorrhage from the lung, the fatal result was not due simply to loss of blood (anæmia), nor to simple occlusion of the air-passages by the extravasated blood, but really to the supervention of œdema—a complication which is explained, on the one hand, by the robust condition of the patient; and, on the other, by the slow course of the hæmorrhage. Not a single ruptured blood-vessel could be discovered.

The conclusions to be drawn from the foregoing statement are as follows:—

1. That death occurred from suffocation caused by pulmonary hæmorrhage and œdema.

2. That no signs of any external injury were revealed by the autopsy.

### CASE II.

A person known. Gunshot wound of head (suicide). Death in twelve hours, or rather more, from œdema of the lungs. On examination post-mortem, the track of the wound found to be through the right hemisphere, and involving the extra-ventricular part of the corpus striatum. Extensive œdema and interstitial emphysema of the lung. Numerous manifestations of older affections; irregularly shaped cranium; unsymmetrically formed brain; contracted aorta; endocarditis mitralis; herpes zoster; chylification going on in the intestines.

B. W., aged twenty-one, a tradesman's assistant, had shot himself through the head with a pocket-pistol above the middle of the left eyebrow. Quite insensible when brought to the Charité at 6 a.m.; breathing stertorous; pulse scarcely perceptible; urine passed involuntarily; loud tracheal râles; heart-sounds scarcely audible; no albumen or sugar in the urine; the left pupil larger than the right. From time to time a whitish greasy matter, mixed with blood, exudes from the small wound. At midday the pulse had somewhat risen; the respiration was still stertorous, though a little easier. In the afternoon the man's condition rapidly changed for the worse, and he died at four o'clock.

Post-mortem examination (occupying two hours and three-quarters), Nov. 3, 1875 :—

### A. *External Examination.*

1. Body generally well-developed; appears to be that of a man of twenty years of age; height, 1·7 metre.

2. Anterior surface generally pale, but the left half of the face, the left ear, the adjacent part of the neck, the arms and forearms, and the thighs and legs much discoloured, and exhibiting large, bluish-red, irregularly shaped spots, of varying size, generally more marked on the left side; but on those parts of the back which have not been exposed to pressure the discoloration is uniform and of a deeper red. On pressing firmly with the finger the redness almost entirely disappears: on an incision being made, a few large drops of semi-fluid blood escape from the skin and subcutaneous tissue, but there are nowhere any permanent reddened patches, such as cannot be removed by water. There is one place on the left thigh, a hand's-breadth above the patella, where, on incision, we find a

small spot extending through the adipose layer, and infiltrated with blood which cannot be pressed out. On the right shoulder-blade there are a few dry, brownish-red spots running obliquely from above, and externally in a direction downwards and inwards. These on section appear to be only thin dry crusts involving the corium proper.

3. On turning the body over, a large quantity of yellowish brown fluid, containing dark-brown particles, escapes from the mouth.

4. Rigor mortis marked in the extremities and in the muscles of the neck and abdomen.

5. Numerous greyish-brown spots—not to be removed by washing—on the anterior surface of the body, especially on the breast. On the left side, near the seventh, eighth, and ninth ribs, there is a broader zone of these spots; this is continued to the arm, where the patches are brownish, and covered with thick masses of epithelium. Other parts, also, of the surface of the body, especially the lower extremities, are covered with grey spots, completely removable by washing. Blackish marks on many parts of the face, neck, arms, and trunk: some of a larger size on the abdomen; these appear, on section, to extend no further than the cuticle.

6. A few pale-greenish faint spots on the abdomen and in the neighbourhood of the groins. Cadaveric odour not perceptible.

7. Hairs dark brown, on right side stained red; much matted together, and their roots covered with dry blood.

8. On the forehead, a finger's-breadth above the middle of the left eyebrow, a small hole three millimetres in diameter, surrounded by a dry, blackish-brown, somewhat depressed border of skin, one to two millimetres broad, around which externally and towards the left side the integument is slightly reddened, and the cuticle abraded. The parts surrounding the wound are slightly swollen. A *long transverse* incision carried down to the bones shows

extensive separation of the connections of the tendinous expansion and the subjacent connective tissue, extending in one spot to the periosteum, and corresponding with a hole in the bone. There is here a flat splintered piece of bone, triangular in shape, five millimetres long, four millimetres wide, retained in its place. The separation thus caused in the parts forms no regular cavity; the wound is traversed by numerous projecting filaments and crossbands of tissue. For five centimetres around this the soft parts are infiltrated with blood, which cannot be pressed out. The tissues for some distance beyond this contain a watery fluid.

9. Eyelids open; corneæ firm and transparent.

10. Nostrils filled with a great quantity of dried blood, which also covers the adjacent parts of the skin.

11. Mouth slightly open at its middle. Lips somewhat red. The teeth closely shut.

12. No other foreign bodies discovered in the apertures of the head.

13. A pale streak on the neck, three millimetres broad, over the larynx, increasing towards the left side to a breadth of fifteen millimetres, and terminating here under the ear; neither a groove, nor injury of the surface, nor any change of colour to be perceived. There is nothing of the kind to be seen on the right side. The skin and subcutaneous tissue quite pale on section.

14. Thorax somewhat flat.

15. Abdomen somewhat retracted.

16. Penis small; much contracted; very little prepuce. The glans and what remains of the prepuce dark red and rather dried. The scrotum likewise small and much wrinkled; externally on both sides some appearance of blood. On incision the integuments of these parts dry superficially and very red.

*17. Anus closed.*

B. *Internal Examination.*— I. *The Cranial Cavities.*

18. Scalp divided by an incision across from one ear to the other, and reflected forwards and backwards. A few drops of blood seen emerging from the anterior portion— these more numerous posteriorly; in front also a close network of distended vessels in the aponeurosis and pericranium. No other spots of extravasated blood, with the exception of those mentioned (in No. 8) in the left frontal region.

19. The aperture mentioned in No. 8 is now seen more distinctly; but there are no fissures surrounding it, and no increase in the quantity of blood in the periosteal vessels.

20. The skull-cap is now removed, the saw being carried horizontally round below the aperture. The bones are difficult to saw through, and on being removed are found to be almost entirely composed of compact substance, and six or even seven or eight millimetres thick. The left frontal sinus is filled with pulpy matter, consisting of whitish, soft, brain-like substance, and dark-red clots, which are partly separable. The right frontal sinus is empty. No fissures are visible in the bones forming the sinuses; but the vessels, as far as they can be made out with the naked eye, are much distended with blood. The external opening (the transverse diameter of which in the outer table is eight millimetres, the diameter from above downwards being six millimetres) has an irregularly hexagonal shape, and leads directly into the left frontal sinus. In this sinus there is another opening, having the same direction, and passing through the inner table just above the orbital plate. This opening is almost completely closed by fragments of cerebral matter and clots of blood; after these are cleared away, a somewhat irregular, but here rather triangular, opening is found, the sides averaging *six millimetres.* At the upper part, and close to the *opening,* there are two larger and two smaller scales of

one, splintered off from the inner table; these are, owever, still loosely connected with the bone.

21. The form of the skull is seen on section to be omewhat oblique, the right half becoming wider posriorly, the left narrower in front. On the left side there s incipient obliteration of the coronal, as well as of the pheno-parietal suture. The right lambdoidal suture is ompletely obliterated. On removing the pericranium, ecent red osseous deposits on various parts of the surface f the skull, especially numerous on the posterior upper art of the temporal ridge. The inner surface of the alvaria dotted over with numerous large pits, principally n the neighbourhood of the anterior fontanelle.

22. The dura mater everywhere thin and diaphanous, xcept in the neighbourhood of the longitudinal sinus, here it is of a dull whitish colour, and traversed by umerous red vessels. On the left side, in front of the anterior art of the brain, there is an aperture in the dura mater, ery irregular in shape, out of which protrude soft roken-up masses of brain substance, mixed with blood; hese are continuous with the previously mentioned *débris* a the aperture in the skull. The opening in the dura ater is on an average from six to seven millimetres wide; s margins are somewhat dentate and wrinkled. There is o blood extravasated anywhere else between the dura ater and the bone.

23. The superior longitudinal sinus anteriorly narrow nd empty; posteriorly, rather wide, and filled with dark emi-fluid blood.

24. On the right side, the dura mater much distended y a bluish mass, which gleams through it. The arteries E the dura mater filled with blood as far as their small amifications, and projecting considerably above the surace of the membrane.

25. On separating the dura mater on the right side, a large clot of blood, dark-coloured, is found to overlay the whole right hemisphere of the brain. It is slightly moist; its own weight causes it to slide from its position ; and it amounts in quantity to twenty-five cubic centimetres. Some portions adhere pretty firmly to the surface both of the dura mater and of the pia mater. On washing the parts with water, the source of the hæmorrhage is found in an aperture in the brain, situated nearly at the posterior part of the middle lobe, two fingers'-breadth behind the end of the fissure of Sylvius ; clots of blood protrude from this opening. The pia mater all around this spot is infiltrated with blood, especially at the anterior perforated spot ; also to a less degree in the sulci of the middle and posterior lobes, and to some extent in those of the anterior lobe.

26. At the anterior extremity of the right anterior lobe, close to the falx cerebri, the pia mater appears more thickly and deeply infiltrated. This appearance is not connected with those above described ; it is more marked inferiorly and in front, where, at the same time, the consistence of the cerebral substance is softer and more yielding.

27. A third, apparently also independent spot, is quite close to the longitudinal fissure at the top of the vertex, under a somewhat thickened part of the pia mater ; it projects somewhat, and is surrounded by a quantity of fluid blood, which spreads also freely towards the dura mater.

28. The head being raised and drawn forward, a leaden bullet, measuring in one direction eight, in the other six millimetres, falls from the parts described in No. 25. This bullet is quite flattened, and bright on one side.

29. Sulci of brain on right side very deep ; perceptible bevelling off of the convolutions just behind the vertex.

). The dura mater being removed on the left side,
d is found effused on the surface in much less
atity; it is, however, equally coagulated, and is more
rent to the membranes, especially to the dura mater.
pia mater infiltrated with blood, but only to a slight
nt, anteriorly near the spot where the external
ing touches the brain, the infiltration extending no
her than a finger's-breadth towards the base, and not
e so far towards the convexity of the brain. A clot of
d eleven millimetres long and five millimetres thick in
aall depression of the surface close by the side of the
cerebri, on the margin of the longitudinal fissure at
vertex; this extends a finger's-breadth further back-
ls than towards the right side. All around the spot
vessels are much distended, and posteriorly the pia
er infiltrated with blood.

. There is, in addition, an extravasation of blood in
low layers between the falx cerebri and the projecting
of the left hemisphere, amounting in quantity to
cely a teaspoonful.

!. The left hemisphere of the brain also appears
essed; the surface of the convolutions is even flatter
on the opposite side.

;. The brain being removed, its base is seen to be
trated with blood to an irregular extent; this is
cially marked in the direction from the aperture in
anterior lobe towards the olfactory nerve, at the
rior part of the middle lobe, around the infundibulum,
ir as the pons Varolii, and even in places as far as the
alla oblongata. The blood for the most part is con-
id in the meshes of the pia mater, but in several
es there are clots obviously non-adherent.

. The pia mater delicate throughout, its vessels filled
blood up to the smaller branches.

35. The brain itself appears shorter, and the convolutions more simple, on the left side than on the right. The consistence good, with the exception of those spots already mentioned.

36. Behind the above-mentioned (No. 22) opening in the dura mater, corresponding to the aperture in the bone, and which is just below the anterior part of the left anterior lobe, there is also a large perforation in the pia mater, fourteen to eighteen millimetres in circumference. Beneath this there is a funnel-shaped excavation, surrounded by soft *débris* of brain-substance, and a few large clots of blood. An oblique incision being made, extending from this spot transversely across to the opening (mentioned in No. 25) in the outer part of the right hemisphere, a continuous canal is exposed : this has a total length of thirteen centimetres, and extends through the middle of the brain-substance, particularly through the base of the corpus striatum, and has a diameter anteriorly of twelve millimetres, posteriorly of eighteen millimetres ; it is filled with coagulum and copious *débris* of brain-matter. The wall of the canal is soft throughout, formed directly of brain-substance, and dotted over with numerous spots of extravasated blood.

37. The point on the vertex of the right hemisphere (described in No. 27) turns out to be a sanguineous infiltration of the pia mater, five millimetres deep. Nothing abnormal found below the other spot particularly referred to in No. 26.

38. The cerebral ventricles are empty, the choroid plexus and the large vessels of the walls of the ventricles filled with blood. The upper vessels of the velum delicate and transparent.

39. Optic thalamus and corpus striatum pale, but not dry.

40. The white substance of the hemispheres is pale and
y; in a few places only, blood escapes from the divided
ssels. The grey substance for the most part pale, but in
aces reddened to some depth.

41. The fourth ventricle is empty; the cerebellum gene-
lly pale, but less so on the left side, where the grey
.bstance is somewhat reddened; and the white substance
)pears to be more infiltrated with a watery fluid.

42. The pons is pale and firm, as is also the medulla
)longata.

43. In the posterior fossa of the base of the skull a large
1antity of fluid blood has collected during the examina-
on; this has escaped from the large blood-vessels of the
:rtebral canal.

44. The transverse sinus almost empty. In the middle
)ssa of the base of the skull, on the left side, the dura
.ater much covered with blood.

45. On removing the dura mater, it is found that several
:ssures of the inner table extend from the opening in the
:ull (No. 19, 20) to the orbital plate. The cracks are
lled with coagulated blood, but they extend for a distance
: only seventeen to eighteen millimetres in a backward
irection.

## II. *Thorax and Abdomen.*

46. A continuous incision, carried as directed from the
hin to the pubic symphysis, and the abdominal cavity
rst laid open. Abdominal organs in their normal position.
he intestines lie very far back. No foreign body in
bdomen. The parts exposed of a pale colour generally;
nly the small intestines slightly reddened.

47. The diaphragm on both sides reaches the lower
order of the fifth rib.

### a. Thorax.

48. The sternum having been removed as directed, the lungs recede very slightly from the wall of the thorax; their anterior portions distended with air, and buoyant, much reddened in places. Between the lobules there are rows of large air-bubbles; and in some spots these coalesce, and form large, continuous level patches.

49. The left lung is free throughout. The pleural sac contains, at a rough guess, forty-five cubic centimetres of a thin, watery liquid, of a dirty-red colour.

50. On the right side the upper parts of the lungs are somewhat bound down by connective tissue; at the base and back part of the pleural cavity there is a very minute quantity of fluid of a similar kind to that found on the other side.

51. The heart, just the size of the man's closed fist, is very rigid, and somewhat flattened on its anterior aspect and over the right auricle. The coronary arteries empty; the coronary veins distended only in their primary ramifications, and somewhat deeply placed. Only a small amount of fat about the pericardium, on which there are a few small detached spots of a deep-red colour, scarcely as large as a millimetre.

52. About forty cubic centimetres of dark blood, for the most part fluid, containing a small buffy clot, escapes from the right auricle. The right ventricle contains blood of a similar kind, dark-red in colour, not more than twenty cubic centimetres, with very faint traces of coagula. In the left auricle the quantity of blood amounts to thirty cubic centimetres, and it is more coagulated and as dark, with a few spots of a faint buffy colour. On the other hand, only a very slight clot with a gelatinous buffy coat occupies the left ventricle.

53. The aorta so narrowed as only to be capable of admitting the tip of the ring-finger. The pulmonary

ery only a little more capacious. A stream of water
ng poured in, none passes into the ventricles. Valves
both sides thin; not discoloured by blood. Narrowing
the mitral valve, which will not admit of two fingers,
.sed by thickening, contraction, and adhesion of the
ι of the valve posteriorly. Muscular tissue much
ənuated, of a brownish-red colour.

4. On the left lung rows of air-vesicles in great abun-
ιce (as described in No. 48) on the lower part of the
erior border, and at the tongue of the upper lobe, and
ι in various places at the lower border of the lung at
 base. Posteriorly, both lobes appear to contain but
le air, and are of a tolerably uniform bluish-red colour;
 lower lobe somewhat greyish-white, owing to thicken-
and serous infiltration, here and there, of the investing
nbrane. Numerous small, slightly raised patches of
ravasated blood scattered about over both lobes.

5. A large quantity of thick bloody froth escapes from
 left bronchus. On cutting through the lung, entire
tions appear red and filled with frothy liquid, but in
er respects unchanged.

6. The same appearances are found on the right side,
 the rows of air-vesicles are less numerous. On the
ər hand, all parts of the lung contain serous exudation,
 the lung-tissue is of a deep-red colour.

7. The tongue, retracted behind the jaws, is covered
h a dirty brown coating, but normal in other respects.
ιe bloody mucus in the pharynx. Both tonsils very
;e, projecting almost like tumours, and seen on section
contain friable masses in the follicles; parenchyma
ιh increased.

8. Veins of the neck filled with dark fluid blood.
eries empty. Nerves normal.

9. Œsophagus contains only a small quantity of light
wnish matter.

ℝ

60. Epiglottis slightly compressed laterally; glottis open. Larynx and air-passages filled with thick frothy fluid, containing a few yellowish-brown flakes. These being removed, the mucous membrane of the upper part is seen to be traversed by an open network of vessels. In the lower parts the vascular network is close, and of a deep-red colour.

61. Aorta narrow, walls thin; contains only fluid blood. The superior vena cava has similar contents.

### b. Abdomen.

62. The spleen is 14·5 centimetres in length, 10 centi-metres in its greatest breadth, and 2·7 centimetres in its greatest thickness; it is very flabby, and somewhat wrinkled. On section, blood exudes from a few large vessels. The Malpighian corpuscles are unusually large, reaching even 1 millimetre in diameter. Splenic pulp scanty and brownish-red.

63. Left kidney 10 centimetres long, 4·5 centimetres broad, 2·9 centimetres thick; flabby; capsule easily sepa-rable; surface smooth, of a dark brownish-red colour; veins easily distinguishable. The tissue on section very dark red; Malpighian corpuscles very prominent, but no other change.

64. Left supra-renal capsule firm; cortical substance slightly developed, medullary substance more so.

65. Right kidney 9·2 centimetres long, 4 centimetres broad, 2·5 centimetres thick; in other respects, as on the left side.

66. Right supra-renal capsule resembles left one.

67. Bladder not much distended. Urine clear, and amounting to about 80 cubic centimetres. Bladder normal.

68. A little clear fluid in both tunicæ vaginales. The substance of the testicles pale but normal.

69. The stomach somewhat distended, its pyloric portion contracted; the veins on the external aspect but slightly distended, and only the larger ones manifest; its general aspect pale. It contains about 150 cubic centimetres of a greenish, thick fluid. The mucous membrane of the fundus is stained greenish-yellow, in the other parts pale red, and towards the pylorus somewhat granulated.

70. The small intestine is contracted almost throughout its extent, only the most deeply situated portions are somewhat distended, and contain liquid. On the external aspect the large veins appear very full, as also some lacteal vessels in the upper portions of the bowel.

71. The mesenteric glands small and slightly reddened. Mesentery loaded with fat.

72. The upper part of the duodenum contains a whitish fluid; lower down, the contents are decidedly yellow. On pressing the gall-bladder, greenish-yellow bile flows freely from the orifice of the gall-duct. Pancreas pale; normal.

73. On opening the jejunum it is found to contain some light grey matter, here and there yellowish and consistent; in its lower portion some thinner fluid deeply tinged with bile. The ileum is almost empty, and contains only a few greenish, tolerably consistent fæcal lumps.

74. The large intestine contains pulpy, greenish-brown fluid masses, mixed with hard fragments, as far as the descending colon; in this latter portion, consistent and formed fæces.

75. Mucous membrane of the jejunum very thick; the villi in the upper part enlarged and milky from absorption of chyle. Lower down, marked reddening of the valvulæ conniventes as far as the place where the contents are coloured with bile; the mucous membrane here becomes also deeply bile-coloured. Lower down, and as far as the beginning of the ileum, the villi are faintly red. Peyer's patches slightly injected, and the glands enlarged in the

lower portion of the ileum. There is also enlargement of the solitary glands close to the ileo-cæcal valve.

76. The mucous membrane of the large intestine very pale, and only in the lower part of a greenish-grey colour.

77. Liver about seventeen centimetres from front to back, twenty-three centimetres broad, and eight centimetres thick; externally greyish-red; smooth and tense; on section, very uniformly reddened, but only a small quantity of blood escapes on the whole, and that merely from the larger vessels. Acini scarcely perceptible, but on closer examination they are seen to be surrounded by a faint light grey bile.

78. Gall-bladder filled with a somewhat ropy, but otherwise clear, dark grey gall.

79. Inferior vena cava moderately distended with blood, for the most part fluid.

This case is a truly remarkable example of the tolerance exhibited by the brain towards injuries of the gravest character. It seems almost miraculous that any one could possibly live twelve hours with a gunshot wound extending from the left frontal region and the apex of the anterior lobe to the external aspect of the middle lobe on the right side (just above the parietal eminence), completely traversing, therefore, in an oblique direction, the right hemisphere of the brain, and also the extra-ventricular part of the corpus striatum. It is only to be accounted for by the smallness of the projectile, and to some extent, also, perhaps, by the slight force which it possessed. The projectile must have been about the size of a pea (five millimetres in diameter), judging from an unused bullet which was found upon the man. The width of the track of the wound in the brain (anteriorly twelve, posteriorly eighteen millimetres) is therefore quite out of proportion to the width of the aperture of entrance in the integument (three millimetres), and in the bones (six to eight millimetres), and also to the projectile. There can, therefore, be no doubt that the track of the wound in the brain was originally much narrower, and that the width which it finally attained was due to the increasing effusion of blood. The symptoms, therefore, of compression of the brain gradually developed as the extravasation increased.

That the force of the projectile was very slight is evident from the fact that not only was there no injury to the bone in the neighbourhood of its place of exit from the brain, but there was even no laceration of the dura mater. The force of the bullet, primarily weak, was still further reduced by its having traversed two layers of bones in its passage through the left frontal sinus; and, on the other hand, the fact that both blood and cerebral matter found an exit through the frontal sinus may well have assisted to retard the development of the symptoms of compression. It thus happened that death resulted not from the brain primarily, but (in a medico-legal sense) from the lung, and, strictly speaking, was due to suffocation. Just as so often occurs in injuries to the head caused by contusion, a fatal œdema of the lung became developed in consequence of the pressure of the extravasated blood upon the medulla oblongata. How greatly the respiration was affected is shown by the interstitial emphysema, which was more extensive in this case than I have ever seen it in the asphyxia of cholera. We should notice, by the way, a combination in itself so very unusual, for, according to current notions, œdema and interstitial emphysema ought strictly to exclude each other.

The widespread indications that the digestive process had not yet terminated, allow us to suppose that the suicide had taken his last meal shortly before the commission of the deed. In addition to this, there are various appearances, which I have grouped together in the summary, indicating the occurrence, in a very early stage, of numerous natural deficiencies, which amply warrants us in drawing conclusions as to the psychological development. The chlorotic condition of the aorta, which may well be connected with the endocarditis mitralis, certainly not very common in so young a man; the obliquity of the cranium, together with the want of symmetry and somewhat defective formation of the brain, are all of them appearances well worthy of observation.

If there were any doubt about the case, and had it been made the subject of legal inquiry, we might summarise our opinions provisionally as follows:—

(1.) That death resulted from œdema of the lung, consequent upon a gunshot wound of the brain.

(2.) That there is no evidence from the autopsy to contradict the assumption that the deceased came to his death by his own hand.


## CASE III.

A person known (suicide). Gunshot wound of the chest. Death occurring in twelve days. Double pleuritis, pericarditis and myocarditis, phlegmonous mediastinitis, exudative peritonitis.

F. K., a tradesman's assistant, twenty years of age, shot himself in the chest, on the afternoon of November 8, with a revolver held at a distance of six inches from his breast, he at the time having nothing on but his shirt. He was immediately brought to the Charité. The aperture of the wound is close to the left nipple, and measures eight millimetres in diameter; it is filled up with clots of blood, and the parts around are emphysematous. The patient complains of difficulty of breathing, and pain all over the left side, where there is also dulness on percussion over the posterior and inferior parts of the chest, extending to the angle of the scapula, with bronchial expiration. The bullet was found in the back above the eighth rib, at a distance of four fingers' breadth from the vertebral column on the left side, and was removed on the following day. It was conical in shape, eleven millimetres long, and seven millimetres in diameter at its base, quite flattened on one side, especially towards its apex. The opinion of the physicians in charge of the case was, that the bullet had passed in the soft parts outside the chest, and had been stopped by the rib.

On the third day, pain came on quite suddenly in the region of the left colon, with great soreness. Manifest improvement on the subsequent days, but great mental excitement and restlessness. The aperture of the bullet's entrance closes, but inflammation and swelling occur round the opening which has been made in the back. The symptoms of inflammation in the left breast gradually diminish. Bowels somewhat confined. On the eighth day a red-coloured serum commences to escape from the wound in the back, and flows more freely during expiration. At the same time there are evident symptoms of pleuritis on the right side, and also of pericarditis. Increased fever and difficulty of respiration. On the eleventh day a puncture was made in the left side of the thorax, in the fifth intercostal space, in the anterior axillary line, and 900 cubic centimetres of a dirty brownish-red serum evacuated. The respiration then for a short time became easier, but very soon after all the serious symptoms became much aggravated, and the patient died on the thirteenth day.

Post-mortem examination (lasting three hours) Nov. 22, 1875 :—

A. *External Examination.*

1. The body is that of a man of about twenty years of age; the height is 1·68 metre; bony conformation slight; adipose tissue in small quantity; muscles moderately developed.

2. Colour generally pale, faintly yellow; lower part of abdomen greenish. The posterior parts of the body, the head, and trunk generally, and also the extremities, covered with large pale bluish-red spots, interrupted by white

patches where exposed to pressure. The intensity of the
colour of these spots can be only slightly diminished by
pressure.  On an incision being made, numerous small
veins filled with blood can be seen extending from the skin
into the substance of the muscles.  Fluid blood escapes
from these, but there is nowhere any blood extravasated in
the tissue.

3. Slight   cadaveric   odour ;   rigor   mortis   in   the
extremities.

4. Eyelids  half  closed ;  eyeballs  tense ;  corneæ  transparent.

5. No foreign body in nose or auditory meatus.

6. Lips  open ;  teeth  separated—the latter, in the upper
jaw, very irregular.  The tongue lying behind the teeth,
and pale ; the teeth of a brownish hue.  No foreign body
in the mouth.

7. Nothing abnormal to be found about the neck.

8. On the right side of the breast a line of four small
brownish-red crusts, one after the other, but separated by
intervals of various lengths.  The first of these is over the
fifth rib, the second over the sixth, the third and fourth
are over the seventh.  The upper one begins a finger's
breadth below the right nipple, and at about the same
distance on its inner side.  The whole line is ten centimetres in length ; its direction is somewhat obliquely
downwards and outwards.  On cutting into these spots
there is neither deposit, tumefaction, nor redness.  On
cutting through them there are no spots of blood, but only
desiccated patches, extending in the highest crust through
the whole thickness of the corium, in the others only
through its most superficial layers.  There is a faint, quite
superficial, crescentic, red spot rather more than a thumb
breadth on the outer side of the right nipple.  This, on
being cut through, is found to involve only the outermost
layers of the corium.  There are also a few more brown

arks on the external aspect of the lower part of the
ıorax on the right side.

9. On the left side, two millimetres above the nipple,
ıt within the areola, a small round spot about 1·5 milli-
etre in diameter, somewhat depressed, of a dirty
·ownish colour, and covered with a dry pellicle. When
.is is cut into, a somewhat hard cord, traversed by
ımerous small vessels filled with blood; and showing
inute spots of blood, is found to extend obliquely out-
ards and backwards through the substance of the gland
to the subcutaneous fat. No canal can be discovered,
ıt in a direction outwards and downwards there are some
attered spots, slightly moist, and blackish-red in colour,
·th in the subcutaneous adipose tissue and in the pectoral
uscles, extending down to the ribs, in a circumference of
ıout seven centimetres. They are most strongly marked
  the direction towards the axilla, where a few of these
nguineous infiltrations extend to the lymphatic glands.
ıese latter are enlarged, hard, bluish-red externally. On
ing cut through they are found to be very moist, and the
ıole of their cortical layers of a dark bluish-red colour.

10. Posteriorly, on the left side of the chest, at a
stance of two fingers' breadth from the middle line, on
e tubercle of the ninth rib, the skin is separated from
e subjacent parts, and exhibits a wound with sharply
fined edges. The wound is four centimetres long and
·o centimetres and a half wide, taking almost the exact
rection of the rib—viz., from within and above, out-
ırds and downwards. It is covered with slightly dull
eyish-red serum, and looks quite clean where this latter
.s been removed ; it penetrates the soft parts in a terrace-
:e form to a depth of eight millimetres, and terminates in
e muscles. The base of the wound is pale and smooth in
e external portion ; internally it is covered with a soft,
lvety, very red film, which contrasts distinctly with the
·ighbouring parts. Only in an upward direction is there

any bloody infiltration of the muscular tissue seen on incision being made into the parts around.

11. On cutting more deeply into the muscular layers lying externally, we come into a shallow cavity which communicates by a narrow opening with the base of the wound above described; it measures four centimetres and a half transversely, and three centimetres perpendicularly; its outer surface is tolerably smooth, and, like the base of the external wound, covered with a similar soft, velvety, red membrane. On opening this cavity, the body being placed on its side, air emerges from beneath with an audible sound, and a small round opening not quite two millimetres in diameter is found on the upper part of the base of the cavity. This penetrates deeply the intercostal space between the eighth and ninth ribs, but on introducing a fine probe it cannot be passed directly into the thoracic cavity. The spiral direction of the track of the wound makes it difficult to pass the probe deeply.

12. The two spots described in Nos. 9 and 10 are now connected by means of a free incision carried transversely round the thorax. The muscular septa in the neighbourhood only of the first spot are found to be distended with dark-red serum, but otherwise there is no trace of any connection between the two wounds.

13. Four fingers' breadth external to and below the left nipple there is a roundish opening, scarcely one millimetre in diameter; the borders of this wound are sharp and rather dry. On incisions being made in various directions, dark-red bloody discolorations are found in the corium below this opening, and these are continuous with those described under No. 9. (This is the aperture of the puncture as stated by the assistant-physician in charge, Dr. N.) No distinct canal can be traced inwards from this opening. On the other hand, on cutting somewhat more deeply into the intercostal muscle, serum and bubbles of

air escape from beneath, and there is a softish, reddish streak to be seen traversing the tissues.

14. Nothing abnormal about the external organs of generation.

15. Anus closed; some fæcal matter round about it.

16. No traces of any other external injury.

B. *Internal Examination.*— I. *Thorax and Abdomen.*

17. An incision is carried from the chin to the symphysis pubis, dividing the integuments of the neck and thorax, and opening the abdominal cavity. Adipose layer slight; muscles of a dull-red colour.

18. The omentum found to be connected by adhesions, which are easily separable, with the anterior part of the abdominal wall and the right border of the liver. This latter organ is somewhat deeply placed, and completely covered by a delicate false membrane, which can be easily stripped off: on the left side it is dry and translucent; on the right side more greasy-looking, dull, and yellowish in colour. The omentum is of a deep-red colour, its veins being particularly full (this most marked on the right side); in the neighbourhood of the gall-bladder it is covered with opaque, yellow false membrane that cannot be stripped off, and this extends as far as the lumbar region.

19. The intestines distended with gas, covered in many places with fine, very superficial, red, vascular networks— generally, however, pale; the viscera of the pelvis only dense bluish-red, with numerous large prominent veins.

20. The pelvis contains about a tablespoonful of slimy, yellowish-red, opaque serum.

### a. The Thorax.

21. During the time that has elapsed since the examination of the wound described in No. 10, a quantity amount-

ing to eighteen cubic centimetres of thin, pale-reddish,
turbid serum, has escaped from this spot into a vessel
placed to receive it.

22. On removing the integuments from the thorax, the
tissues are found to be considerably infiltrated with blood,
on the left side, in the fourth and fifth intercostal spaces;
in the first of these at a distance of three, and in the
second at a distance of two fingers' breadth from the
sternum.

23. On cutting into the wall of the thorax on the right
side, fluid escapes. This is immediately collected from the
pleural sac. It is found to amount to 800 cubic centimetres, is thin, relatively only slightly turbid, and of a
yellowish-red colour. It contains numerous large very
loose flakes, yellowish-white in colour. The surface of the
pleura on this side is everywhere covered with somewhat
soft dirty-yellowish deposit, which can be stripped off.

24. The sternum being removed, the whole of the mediastinum is found to be tough and difficult to cut, many of
its smaller vessels filled with blood, and the tissue throughout of a gelatinous appearance and of a dull brownish-
yellow colour.

25. On the left side, the anterior portion of the lung is
agglutinated to the wall of the thorax for a length of eight
centimetres. After it has been separated we come to a
space filled with fluid. The fluid is ladled out; it measures
900 cubic centimetres, is somewhat thick, but flows freely,
is of a palish-red colour, has a faint odour, and contains a
few flakes. This cavity is the pleural sac, the walls of
which, except where they are agglutinated, are covered
with thick, dirty reddish-yellow, closely adherent deposits,
with red infiltration in some places. The upper and lower
lobes are agglutinated together below. There are also
adhesions which can be easily broken up between the
thoracic wall and the lower part of the upper, and the
*anterior* and lower part of the lower, lobe. These adhe-

sions extend over a surface as large as a child's hand. In front, between the pericardium and lungs, is a closed space, containing large shreds of gelatinous coagula. This cavity is found to be an incapsulated part of the pleural sac.

26. The pericardium much thickened externally. Internally, extensive deposit of rough, stiff, elastic membrane, both on the parietal and visceral layer. The cavity contains about forty cubic centimetres of pale-reddish serum, mixed with yellowish flakes. The firm deposit is most abundant on the anterior portion of the parietal layer; and, corresponding to this, the heart is covered anteriorly by similar false membrane.

27. The heart itself is somewhat larger than the closed fist of the man. It is rigid, its surface slightly arched, comparatively pale in colour. The right auricle contains about ninety cubic centimetres of dark-red coagulated blood. The right ventricle contains a very small quantity of fluid blood, but a few large, gelatinous, buffy masses. The left auricle contains scarcely two tablespoonfuls of dark blood, very slightly coagulated. The left ventricle is almost empty.

28. The heart is then removed. The arterial valves close. On being opened, a marked red infiltration throughout the lining membrane. The muscular tissue firm; on the right side greyish-red; eighteen millimetres thick. On the posterior wall it is closely marked to a depth of eight millimetres with very extraordinary yellow spots and stripes. These spots being immediately subjected to microscopical examination show the primitive muscular fasciculi to be without cross-markings and filled with coarse fat-granules. No other abnormal appearances.

29. A very large quantity of dark, partly buffy coagula escapes from the large vessels of the thorax.

30. The left lung is rather flat, and contains but little

air. Its serous covering on the upper and anterior parts is
thickened, opaque, here and there yellowish; on the inferior and posterior parts of a dull-red colour, softer and
more lubricous, dotted over in several places with soft,
grey, roundish granulations. In three places the covering
of the lung is relatively smooth, and shows scarcely any
deposit. These places are circumscribed by tolerably sharp
edges, with salient and receding angles. There are similar
places corresponding to these on the wall of the chest. The
first of these spots is close to the anterior border of the
upper lobe, near the agglutination described in No. 25.
The second spot is on the lower tongue of the upper lobe.
The surface of the lung is here induplicated in two directions, meeting in an angle, and taking a course toward
the spot immediately to be described. The third spot is on
the lower and anterior aspect of the lower lobe, and here in
a line, one below the other, we find (a) on the surface
turned to the cleft between the upper and lower lobes, one
centimetre from the border, a roundish depression of
reddish colour, three millimetres in diameter, exhibiting
on incision, a perforation of the pleural investment; (b) two
round spots close to one another, two and a half to three
millimetres in diameter; one of which is upon, the other
close in front of, the border. These being cut through, are
found to be yellowish-white channels in the pleural membrane and the adjacent pulmonary tissue. The latter is on
this spot somewhat firmer, and of a deep-red colour to a
depth of eight millimetres. On section the tissue in the
upper lobe is found to contain very little air, is of a red
colour throughout; but it is only from the larger vessels
that any blood escapes. The lower lobe contains still less
air, and is moderately red; dark thick blood escapes from
the vessels.

31. The right lung is covered throughout its whole
extent with firmly adherent but separable deposit; on the
upper and middle lobes the pleural covering is whitish and
*thickened.* On section the tissue is found to contain but

little air, and is somewhat grey in colour; this is the case also in the lower lobe.

32. On the inner aspect of the thoracic wall on the left side, exactly upon the eighth rib, at a distance of four fingers' breadth externally from the vertebral column, there is a solution of continuity, twelve millimetres long and five millimetres wide, of a somewhat long oval form, the long diameter being parallel to the axis of the rib, the borders gradually sloping off, and of a yellowish colour. In the base of this wound the bone lies exposed. In order to examine the parts more closely, this rib and the ninth are removed together, and it is now seen that, at the spot corresponding to the external wound, the inner surface of the eighth rib, for a length of fourteen and a breadth of ten millimetres, is quite laid bare, and the soft parts stripped off. At this spot there are two small linear fragments of lead, the larger three, the smaller one and a half millimetres long, wedged into the compact tissue of the bone. Round the denuded portion of the rib the tissue is raised up like a wall, thickened and much reddened. Beyond this wound, anteriorly, and on the same rib, a triangular, greyish-yellow spot is found on the costal pleura, which exactly corresponds with a similar triangular spot on the inferior lobe of the lung, immediately below the smooth spot described in No. 30, and in the direction of the appearances detailed under (a) and (b) in the same paragraph. A continuous canal connects the denuded portion of bone with the cavity mentioned in No. 11.

33. In the anterior lateral portion of the circumference of the left pleural cavity, in the intercostal space between the fourth and fifth ribs, three centimetres from the attachment of the cartilages, is a deepened cleft, placed transversely to the course of the third rib, seven millimetres long, and rather more than three millimetres wide; running somewhat obliquely from above and within, downwards and outwards, ending above the border of the fifth

rib, and separating the fasciæ superficially. The floor of
this cleft is tolerably smooth, slightly scaly. The borders
of the cleft are sharp, neither thickened nor reddened; in
its base several small, angular, blackish fragments of lead,
are contained in the tissue. This spot corresponds to an
area of the pulmonary pleura, free from deposit, and
which had previously been adherent (No. 25).

34. Lower down in the intercostal space, between the
fifth and sixth ribs, and almost exactly in the middle,
there is a somewhat long cleft, with tolerably straight
borders; it is scarcely two millimetres long, and its lateral
edges are close together. It leads directly externally into
a small canal through the muscles. Its position corresponds to the external wound described under No. 13, but
there is no open passage from one to the other.

35. The veins of the neck are tumid, and contain thick
blood; arteries and nerves normal.

36. The œsophagus contains a yellowish-grey fluid, and
numerous fragments of food. Mucous membrane pale.
Palate much reddened, with very prominent venous networks; follicles of the tongue slightly swollen.

37. The larynx contains a few similar yellowish-green
fragments of food. Below, a little frothy liquid in the
air-tubes. Mucous membrane somewhat thick; that of the
air-tubes very red, owing to numerous vascular networks,
which are distinctly visible.

38. No change in the walls of the aorta; only a little
thick blood in its descending portion.

### b. The Abdomen.

39. The spleen adherent on its upper aspect, $12\frac{1}{4}$ centimetres long, $7\frac{1}{2}$ centimetres broad, 3·6 centimetres thick,
firm on section, and pale; the pulp rather greyish-red and
uneven, containing much blood and slightly indurated,

only in a part which is covered externally by dirty lowish-white membrane. Follicles small and grey.

0. Left kidney 12 centimetres long, 5 centimetres ad, 3·2 centimetres thick. The capsule easily sepa-ed; surface smooth, brownish-grey-red in colour, erficial veins slightly distended. On section somewhat eral faintly grey cloudiness of the cortical substance, ich appears bluish-red. The Malpighian corpuscles minent on the cut surface, slightly reddened.

1. The left supra-renal capsule reddish-grey in its ical substance; tissue between it and kidney abundant . full of blood.

2. Right kidney 11 centimetres long, 6 centimetres ad, 3·2 centimetres thick. The surface somewhat more kly red than on the other side. In other respects, the ie appearances both here and in the supra-renal capsule m the other side.

3. Urinary bladder strongly contracted; contains a lespoonful of dark yellowish-brown urine. In other ects normal, as are also the prostate and vesiculæ inales.

4. Testicles, both superficially and in their substance, ewhat bluish-red in colour, owing to numerous veins; ther respects normal.

5. Stomach rather capacious, containing a large quan-· of greenish liquid and numerous fragments of food. cous membrane pale, whitish-grey, tolerably thick, ewhat wrinkled towards the pylorus.

6. The duodenum contains a large quantity of bilious ty fluid. A drop of bile exudes on pressure from the ice of the gall-duct, and also when the gall-bladder is sed.

7. The liver twenty-five centimetres broad, twenty-two imetres from front to back, and eight centimetres

thick; the whole of its external surface covered with yellowish-white false membrane. On incision, the large vessels only found filled with blood. The tissue pretty uniformly brownish-grey, brittle, somewhat dull looking. The acini large, externally yellowish, internally greyish-red. Gall-bladder slightly coloured; bile greyish-brown, with yellow flakes.

48. Pancreas somewhat flabby; its posterior portion infiltrated with blood.

49. The mesenteric glands somewhat enlarged; their cortical portions somewhat white. But little fat about the mesentery.

50. The small intestine contains a large quantity of pasty, bilious matter; in the lower portion the contents are fæculent and foul-smelling. The mucous membrane is rather thick; in the jejunum reddened only in a few spots; a few turgid veins in other places. The only change in the glands is a very slight swelling of the solitary follicles in the lower part of the ileum.

51. The large intestine contains soft fæces; mucous membrane rather thick; some difficulty in removing the adherent fæces; nothing abnormal.

## II. *The Cranium.*

52. The soft parts cut through according to the directions, and reflected backwards and forwards; nothing abnormal.

53. The skull of a somewhat long oval form, much reddened posteriorly, and presenting a pitted depression on the frontal bone, just in front of the coronal suture, and to the right of the mesial line. On section, diploe scanty but red. Bones of skull four millimetres thick. Internal surface somewhat irregular in consequence of various depressions in the middle part of the frontal bone and

along the sagittal suture; these are apparently due to elevations of the pia mater.

54. The dura mater translucent, thickened, and copiously supplied with blood in the middle and anterior portion. The longitudinal sinus rather large, filled with buffy coagula. Inner surface of the dura mater on both sides smooth, exhibiting in places networks of distended vessels, but no abnormal deposit.

55. The surface of the cerebral hemispheres symmetrical in shape. The convolutions rather large. Veins very large, much distended with dark blood, particularly at the back of the head.

56. Pia mater everywhere translucent, exhibiting large wart-like excrescences along the median longitudinal fissure and under the frontal bone.

57. Scarcely any fluid in the lateral ventricles. Posterior cornua obliterated. Choroid plexus and vessels of the velum of a dark-red colour.

58. On section the cerebral hemispheres found to be very moist, and the veins much distended. From these latter large drops of blood exude all over the cut surface. Grey substance shining and of a dark reddish tinge.

59. The grey substance of the large ganglia reddened; the tissue very moist throughout. Corpora quadrigemina pale.

60. Fourth ventricle empty. Cortical portion of cerebellum uniformly reddened; veins of medullary substance distended.

61. The arteries at the base of the brain regular in their course, filled with dark blood. In the pia mater of this part nothing abnormal.

62. The grey substance of the pons Varolii and medulla oblongata slightly reddened.

63. The sinuses at the base of the skull filled with dark

thick blood. The dura mater thin and delicate. Condition of the bones normal.

There is much that is worthy of remark about this case. Apart from the fact that the extensive peritonitis did not occur as a clinical symptom (we must now regard as such the pain in the region of the left colon, which was noticed on the third day of the disease, but which afterwards quite subsided), the rapidity with which death occurred must obviously be explained by the pericarditis and the resulting myocarditis. Some time ago (in my *Archiv*, 1858, vol. xiii. page 266) I reported several cases of malignant pericarditis, in which I demonstrated acute fatty metamorphosis of the muscular tissue, and showed that the morbid process advanced from without to within. I have several times since observed this very dangerous complication, of which the case before us is another and a very instructive example.

The peritonitis, and also the pericarditis, and the pleural inflammation on the right side, have no immediate connection with the wound caused by the bullet. The probability is that all of these are the result of the phlegmonous mediastinitis, which in this case quite takes the form of a malignant erysipelas. The occurrence, however, of this mediastinitis is not a little extraordinary, for the bullet did not immediately injure the mediastinum; and, moreover, the anterior portion of the track of the bullet showed no indications of mischief, for it was completely closed by the first intention. There is, therefore, nothing else but to assume that all these morbid processes have extended themselves from the posterior part of the track, which was certainly in an unhealthy condition, and which was converted into a perforating wound when the bullet was excised. It is, therefore, very extraordinary that when the examination was made there was no disagreeable odour about the opening in the back.

Notwithstanding this, however, a propagation of infectious matter from this quarter is indicated by the extensively diseased appearance of the left pulmonary pleura, and the alterations so unusually great for so comparatively short a period as twelve days. The pleura was so thickened, dull, and wrinkled, and so dotted over posteriorly with real sprouting granulations, and in large area almost trachomatous, as to present an appearance such as is only met with in very malignant forms of inflammation. Those portions of the pleura primarily agglutinated appeared, after separation, both on the lung and on the wall of the chest, so smooth and delicate that they looked quite normal when contrasted with what has just been described.

The autopsy has not confirmed the supposition that this was a case in which the bullet, in consequence of the retracted position of the left side of the chest, took a curved direction through the external soft parts from the place of entrance near the nipple, until it was stopped posteriorly by the eighth rib. Certainly, it appeared at first as if the sanguineous infiltrations (No. 9) extending to the axilla corresponded with the course taken by the bullet. But the further examination showed that the bullet had taken an entirely opposite direction, and that the infiltrations were caused only by the loose cellular tissue being filled with blood in the direction of the lymph-current. Even the axillary glands were so infiltrated with blood as to prove distinctly that their appearance was due to absorption. I draw particular attention to this, inasmuch as I am well aware that in medico-legal practice due regard is not paid during life to this form of propagation of sanguineous infiltrations, so very important, and yet so often misleading, owing to the great possibility of a false interpretation.

The shot has entered just above the left nipple, and taken an oblique direction outwards, downwards, and backwards; it has left the wall of the chest, first of all, in the fourth intercostal space, and then entered the pleural cavity; it has then grazed the lung, but only a small portion of it—viz., the surface of the left lower lobe turned towards the cleft between the two lobes; it has

then passed over the internal surface of the eighth rib,
at a distance of four fingers' breadth from the vertebral
column, and close to this spot perforated the eighth intercostal space.  Here it remained lying in the soft parts
under the skin of the back until its early removal.

Strange to say, at the end of the channel of entrance,
just where it passes obliquely over the upper border of the
fifth rib, several small pieces of lead, obviously portions
of the bullet, were found covered up in the soft parts.
At the first glance, they might be compared with the
fragments of lead embedded in the bone, at the posterior
part of the circumference of the thorax, where the rib has
been laid bare by the bullet.  However, a closer examination proves that their origin is different.  The latter were
obviously splintered off when the bullet struck against the
rib, and they correspond probably to the small scratches
found on the smooth compressed surface of the much-
flattened bullet.  The former, on the other hand—those
which are closed up in the anterior wound,—could not
have been splintered off by the rib, for its border, although
very close to the bullet's course, has not been touched by
it.  These must, therefore, have been stripped off previously, perhaps in the grooved barrel of the revolver, and
driven into the wound when the shot was fired.

The medico-legal conclusions in this case are as
follows :—

1. That death was caused by a series of violent inflammatory attacks in the thoracic and abdominal cavities,
inflammation of the heart being the principal factor.

2. That these inflammatory attacks were the result of a
gunshot wound of the thorax.

3. That there is nothing to contradict the assumption
that the fatal shot was fired by the deceased himself.

## CASE IV.

A twin child, still-born at the middle of the tenth (lunar) month. Indications of immaturity. Inflammatory œdema (erysipelas) of the scrotum, pharynx, and brain. Incipient white hepatisation of the lungs.

The case is peculiarly interesting from the fact that the other child was born alive and throve well, and that the mother, to all appearances, had never suffered from syphilis or from any puerperal affection.

Post-mortem examination (lasting one hour and a half), December 13, 1875 :—

### A. *External Examination.*

1. The body is that of a new-born male child, and is 46 centimetres in length, 2,120 grammes in weight; for the most part regularly formed, though the limbs are rather short. The subcutaneous fat is moderate in quantity; the muscles somewhat poorly developed. The legs slightly curved.

2. The umbilicus projects about 1½ centimetres, and has the remains of the umbilical cord, properly ligatured, attached to it. This latter is 10½ centimetres in length, and averages 1¼ centimetres in thickness; its extremity presents a flattened surface, the cord itself is rounded, tense, gelatinous, and presents no appearance of dryness.

3. The colour of the body is generally pale, even over the abdomen; yellowish about the head, of a washy pale red over the back, and likewise (though of a darker red) over the right side of the head and face. Pressure, however, has caused portions of these latter parts, the right external ear especially, to look quite pale. Firm pressure with the thumb causes the greater part of the redness to disappear; on incision, the venous network for

some depth is seen to be filled with blood, and a small quantity of fluid blood escapes.

4. The skin of certain portions of the trunk, especially about the groins, is covered with a white caseous layer.

5. Rigor mortis well marked in the upper extremities and lower jaw ; less marked elsewhere.

6. The head of oblong shape, the occiput rather small. The long diameter 11½ centimetres, the transverse 9½ centimetres, the oblique 11 centimetres. Pretty well covered with short, dark brown hair, up to two centimetres in length, and extending rather far over the forehead and face. The bones of the head are readily movable, somewhat overlapping each other, the right parietal bone especially projecting over the left. Both fontanelles small, the anterior one 2 centimetres broad, 3½ centimetres long ; the posterior 1 centimetre each way.

7. The eyelids closed. The eyeballs tense, the corneæ slightly cloudy, the pupils large and quite open ; no trace of pupillary membrane.

8. The nasal cartilages firm, the nasal openings free.

9. Mouth closed, upper lip very prominent, both lips slightly red. Tongue behind the jaws, pale reddish. No foreign body in the mouth.

10. Ears large, cartilages deficient in firmness, passages empty.

11. Neck movable, but within the ordinary limits ; nothing abnormal in other respects.

12. Thorax somewhat convex. Circumference at lower part 27 centimetres, measurement across shoulders 1? centimetres.

13. Abdomen flat. Anterior spinous processes 6½ centimetres apart, crests of the ilia 7½ centimetres at greater distance apart.

14. External organs of generation properly formed, both testicles descended. The scrotum pale, swollen, translucent; its subcutaneous tissue on section found to be infiltrated with a deep yellow, watery fluid which escapes in abundance on pressure.

15. Anus closed ; no foreign body present.

16. The finger and toe-nails somewhat soft; the former reaching the tips of the fingers, the latter not extending to the ends of the toes.

17. The cartilaginous layer having been gradually removed, no centre of ossification discoverable in the lower extremity of the right femur. The same deficiency observable on the left side on making a longitudinal incision. At the boundary between the bone and cartilage a small, slightly yellowish layer visible.

18. Incisions having been made into the upper ends of the tibia, fibula, femur, and humerus on both sides, nothing abnormal discovered at the margin of ossification. No formation of nuclei in the epiphyses.

19. No sign of any injury to the body.

B. *Internal Examination.*—I. *Thorax and Abdomen.*

20. The integuments divided by an incision from the chin to the pubic symphysis and carried to the left of the umbilicus ; the abdominal cavity opened. The diaphragm found to correspond to the lower border of the fourth rib.

21. The umbilical vessels almost empty; on incision only a drop of semifluid blood escapes.

22. The liver fills the whole of the epigastric region, so that the stomach is not visible. The large intestine distended by meconium and of a green colour; the greater part of the transverse colon, the cæcum and a loop of the sigmoid flexure prominently visible, but in their normal situation. The interval between the two latter filled by

the much distended bladder. Numerous loops of the small intestines occupy the remainder of the space; these are somewhat flattened from mutual pressure, apparently empty, of a rosy greyish-white colour; a few congested veins to be seen only in the omentum, which is devoid of fat, and in the mesentery. On turning up the liver the stomach is seen to be pale and closely contracted.

23. No foreign body in the abdominal cavity.

### (a.) The Thorax.

24. The trachea having been ligatured in the prescribed manner, and the sternum (still almost entirely cartilaginous) having been removed with the costal cartilages, the thoracic organs are found to be in their regular position. The upper part of the mediastinum is occupied by the very large thymus gland, the left lung is withdrawn behind the pericardium, so that an interval, almost as wide as the little finger, separates the thoracic wall from the latter structure; the right lung covers the lateral portion of the thymus and of the pericardium, and almost all the right portion of the diaphragm.

25. The prominent portions of both lungs present a pale greyish-red, clearly lobulated appearance, the more distinct by reason of the dark congested state of large superficial vessels; in many places the colour is almost yellowish-red. These parts are flabby, and do not crepitate when handled.

26. The pleuræ empty, their surface moist. On the diaphragm, especially on the left side, small, dark-red, injected patches visible.

27. The pericardium contains about half a teaspoonful of a dark brownish-yellow, but clear fluid. The internal surface pale and smooth. The heart somewhat larger than the closed fist of the child, firm, its surface slightly arched, pale in colour; the superficial veins filled with blood up to their roots; the auricles, with their appendages, bluish-red, moderately distended.

28. On incision the right auricle found to contain scarcely a teaspoonful of fluid blood. Also the right ventricle contains only fluid blood, but in less quantity. The left ventricle is almost empty ; about half a teaspoonful of fluid blood in the auricle.

29. The heart is now removed and further incisions made. All the valves are regular in form, of a slightly reddish tinge (from imbibition). The foramen ovale still perfectly open. The muscular tissue pale, somewhat greyish red.

30. Rather less than a teaspoonful of dark fluid-blood escapes from the large vessels of the thorax.

31. The thymus gland is now carefully removed. It is 4½ centimetres broad, 4 centimetres long, and 9 millimetres thick ; greyish-white, medullary-looking in colour, and presenting the same appearance on section.

32. The veins of the neck tumid with dark fluid-blood. The arteries also contain blood of a similar character. The large nerves are pale and apparently normal.

33. The tongue, with the organs of the neck, removed from below, as directed. The posterior portion of the mouth contains no foreign body. The uvula and soft palate found to be much swollen, pale and gelatinous ; on incision a yellowish fluid escapes.

34. The mucous membrane of the epiglottis and aperture of the larynx is similarly, though less, swollen and thickened by watery infiltration ; similar though less decided swelling of the mucous membrane of the pharynx, which part is somewhat reddened throughout, owing to a superficial fine network of vessels.

35. The upper part of the œsophagus contains some yellowish fluid ; mucous membrane decidedly pale.

36. The epiglottis folded together laterally. The glottis very narrow ; larynx and trachea empty, mucous membrane

delicate and thin ; on the softer spots superficial vascular networks visible.

37. After dividing the trachea above the ligature, the remaining thoracic viscera were removed together, and placed in a vessel with water. They were found to sink.

38. The external surface of the lung posteriorly is of a uniform, rather bluish-grey red colour, but without marked congestion of the superficial vessels. The surface of these posterior portions, especially on the left side, is for the most part perfectly smooth. On closer examination no air vesicles are to be seen, but on many of the lobules small whitish-grey racemose marks.

39. Each separate lung sinks in water, as do also separate lobes and small fragments, even from the generally bright-coloured portions of the anterior border.

40. The lower portion of the trachea and its branches are empty but deeply reddened.

41. Incisions being made, the tissue of the lung appears greyish-red, very moist and glossy, and exhibits clusters of small, firm, whitish-grey spots corresponding to the internal parts of the lobules. There is no crepitation, and neither froth nor air-bubbles escape by pressing the sides of the cut surfaces, but only a little clear fluid and a few drops of blood. Even when incised under water no air-bubbles escape from the tissue. The lungs were set aside for microscopical examination.

42. The lower portion of the oesophagus is empty and pale.

43. The aorta contains a little fluid blood ; its internal surface is somewhat reddened. The vessels are given off irregularly from the thoracic portion.

44. The foramen ovale is perfectly open (12 millimetres in circumference), and presents on its anterior wall an oblong, flat, dark greyish-red projection, which on section

is found to consist of coagulated blood deposited in the wall of the heart.

### (b.) *The Abdomen.*

45. The spleen 4·1 centimetres long, 2·2 centimetres in its greatest breadth, 8 millimetres in its greatest thickness; its upper end wrinkled and turned inwards, dark brownish-red in colour, flabby consistence on section, the follicles small; pulp fragile, abundant, brownish-red.

46. The left suprarenal capsule 25 millimetres long, 32 millimetres broad; on section, very vascular, brownish-red almost throughout, the different portions distinguished with difficulty, scarcely any fat in the cortex.

47. The left kidney 50 millimetres long, 20 millimetres broad, 18 millimetres thick. The capsule easily separable, the surface showing deep divisions, but otherwise smooth, pale, and with a faint brownish-red tinge. On section the cortical substance similarly coloured; the medullary substance for the most part greyish-red, without cloudiness or deposit, but of a deeper red in the external portions. A little urine in the pelvis of the kidney and ureter.

48. The same organs on the right side in much the same condition.

49. The urinary bladder contains clear fluid; the mucous membrane pale.

50. Both testicles in the scrotum, of normal size and somewhat bluish-red appearance.

51. The duodenum now opened on its anterior aspect. It is seen to be full of soft pultaceous contents, whitish in colour, with a slight tendency to yellow. The mucous membrane itself is faintly reddened. The papilla of the biliary duct is open and very prominent, and from it a drop of watery bile exudes on pressing the gall-bladder.

52. A thin transparent layer covers the wall of the

stomach; the mucous membrane is thrown into marked longitudinal folds, which exhibit patches of redness. On some of these patches fine vascular networks are visible; other patches are uniformly dark red.

53. Pancreas somewhat firm, pale anteriorly, slightly reddened posteriorly.

54. The liver 10 centimetres broad, 58 millimetres wide, and 22 millimetres in thickness, pretty uniformly reddened, exhibiting at one spot on the anterior surface both of the right and left lobe a flattened extravasation of fluid blood under the capsule. The substance of the organ flabby, uniformly greyish-red on section, turning to a uniform grey after pressing out the blood, which escapes pretty freely. The lobules not clearly recognisable. At the portal fissure, a small whitish firm body, the size of a hemp-seed, is firmly adherent to the capsule of the liver.

55. The mesentery contains many whitish-looking, slightly enlarged, lymphatic glands.

56. The small intestine contains flocculent, pultaceous, slightly yellowish-white, epithelial matters. The ileum is much contracted; its contents are brownish-yellow, feebly resembling meconium, and are more abundant near the ileo-cæcal valve. The large intestine is filled with meconium. The mucous membrane throughout is tolerably thick, faintly reddened, greenish in the parts containing meconium: no other change.

57. The large vessels on the vertebræ are almost empty.


II. *The Cranial Cavities.*

58. The integuments having been divided as directed, and turned aside, are seen to be infiltrated with a yellowish fluid, the infiltration extending to the periosteum. On the right side, especially at the posterior part, there is also a pale reddish infiltration of all the tissues down to the

periosteum. Congestion of the veins up to their small branches. The scalp exhibits in places thick red spots, as large as a flea-bite or a lentil; these, on incision, are found to be the result of uniform sanguinary infiltration.

59. The skull-cap is now sawn through, the dura mater divided, and the brain, which is very soft, removed. A teaspoonful of clear fluid found at the base of the skull, but nothing else abnormal in this part.

60. The bones of the skull relatively thin, movable.

61. On the inner surface of the dura mater, near the coronary suture, there are a few minute red specks of blood in the tissue. The longitudinal sinus contains only fluid blood.

62. The brain itself regularly formed; the pia mater delicate, and containing everywhere very numerous venous networks.

63. After cutting through the hemispheres, each lateral ventricle is found to contain a small quantity of fluid; the lining membrane of these cavities somewhat firm, the veins on the surface congested, as are also those of the velum and choroid plexus.

64. The section through the hemispheres shows a remarkably pale tissue of a peculiar yellowish-white colour, the medullary substance being with difficulty distinguished from the cortex, the only difference being that the latter appears paler and whiter than the former. The medullary substance is also very moist and shining, and of gelatinous appearance. These parts put aside for microscopical examination.

65. The optic thalamus, corpus striatum, and the corpora quadrigemina are pale-yellowish in colour and moist throughout.

66. The cerebellum in the same condition; a few congested veins visible only in the corpus dentatum. The fourth ventricle empty.

67. At the base of the brain, very marked congestion of the veins of the pia mater, especially at the fissure of Sylvius.

68. The pons Varolii somewhat firmer in consistence, pale on section.

69. The medulla oblongata very firm, but at the same time very pale.

70. There are no injuries to the bones at the base of the skull.

On microscopical examination of the lungs we find that the ends of the bronchioles, the infundibula, and the alveoli are completely packed with dense accumulations of epithelial cells, some of which are full of fine, shining granules (myelin). On examining the brain the white substance is found to contain scattered, highly refractile globular granules; the grey substance, numerous pale-grey nucleated cells.

This case presents a series of post-mortem appearances of an extremely singular character. The most important are those which, even at first sight, appeared to be connected together, viz., the œdema of the scrotum, the œdema of the uvula, soft palate, pharynx, and upper parts of the larynx, and likewise the œdema of the brain. All these, parts were found to contain a clear but yellowish fluid abundant in quantity, and removable by pressure; in the brain the yellow colour somewhat less marked, but unusually decided in the scrotum and uvula. There can be no doubt as to the acute nature of these appearances. But what is their import? The absence of venous hyper-æmia in the affected parts is most decisive evidence against attributing the appearances to effusion, the results of passive congestion. We may, however, with some show of truth, refer the symptoms to a general dropsy. If we consider by itself the state of the soft palate, pharynx and larynx, there need be no scruple about designating it as acute laryngo-pharyngeal œdema. This œdema, however, belongs to the class of the so-called active processes; as a

general rule, it is purely an erysipelas. In my work on
"Special Pathology and Therapeutics" (Erlangen, 1854,
vol. i., pp. 209, 217), I have minutely discussed the conditions of this form of œdema, and I can only say that my
subsequent and much-enlarged experience has convinced
me of the relationship between this affection and erysipelas ; or, I should rather say, of the identity of the two
processes. I have repeatedly observed in new-born infants,
even clinically, a primary œdema of the scrotum followed
by acute œdema of the pharynx and larynx, sometimes, indeed, assuming a phlegmonous type. These are
allied branches of that affection which, when it occurs in a
more diffused form, occasionally presents the appearance of
the so-called sclerema, or induration of the cellular tissue
(see my " Gesammelten Abhandlungen," pp. 112, 701).

In the case before us, there are two appearances indicative
of the existence of several general derangements of an
allied kind. The first of these is that peculiar infiltration
of the soft parts of the head with a deeply yellowish
fluid, the signification of which was suggested in the
external examination, and the second is that peculiar,
almost brownish coloration of the pericardial fluid. That
these appearances were not due to post-mortem changes is
evident from the fact that there were no signs of decomposition present.

Very unusual, and likewise very remarkable, is the
œdema of the brain, a condition which was found to be
associated with general paleness of the organ, and marked
fatty metamorphosis of the cells of the neuroglia of the
medullary substance. I have no hesitation in assigning
this condition to the same group as before, and in describing it as acute œdema, or even as erysipelas, of the brain.

Had the mother suffered from puerperal fever, the
further interpretation of the morbid appearances could
have presented less difficulty. But not only was the
mother perfectly healthy, but the other child was free from
all similar symptoms. The fact is, therefore, that the case

is one of a congenital affection which must have become
developed *in utero*. As I have before shown (see my
Archiv., vol. xxxviii. p. 135, 1867; vol. xliv. p. 472, 1873;
Geschwülste, vol. ii. p. 469), fatty metamorphosis of the
white substance of the brain, and more especially, incipient
white hepatisation of the lungs, are very frequently met
with in syphilitic cases. But I have already alluded to the
fact that the mother showed no sign of syphilis, and
although syphilis in the father was not excluded by such
evidence, there was no real support for such an assumption.
Besides, as I have before mentioned, both the conditions in
question occur in new-born children, free from any
suspicion of syphilis. We cannot therefore go farther into
the question of causation. The case may be provisionally
described as a rare example of congenital erysipelas,
involving visceral, as well as external, organs.

From a legal point of view the case is extremely interesting, not only because, in an otherwise viable child, death
was the result of such latent morbid processes, but also
from the fact that there were such extraordinary signs of
immaturity in a child of the tenth month. Not only were
the nails imperfectly developed, and the cartilages of the
ears very delicate and movable, but there was no trace of
any centre of ossification in the inferior epiphysis of the
femur. We have, it is true, other observations with reference to this defect: I refer especially to G. Hartmann's
"Dissertation" (Beiträge zur Osteologie der Neugeborner,
Tübingen, 1869, p. 18). So complete a defect, however, in
the ossification of the extremities (and in the sternum)
co-existing with the advanced stage of the same process in
the bones of the skull, is well worthy of attention.

The case well illustrates the importance of microscopical
examination for the decision of medico-legal questions, for
by this means we were enabled to detect changes both in the
brain and lungs. Owing to the proliferation of epithelium
in the infundibula and alveoli, the lungs appeared so
bright-red in colour, that I was at first inclined to believe

that respiration had taken place. But on very close examination I noticed that the air-cells were occluded, and my observation was confirmed by the microscope.

The medico-legal conclusions to be drawn in this case would be as follows :—

1. The body was that of a new-born child.

2. The question whether the child was of the full term or not, could not positively be determined by the examination.

3. Respiration had not taken place, either during or after birth.

4. The child was not capable of living out of the womb of its mother; its death *in utero* was caused by disease implicating the lungs, larynx, and brain.

5. There were no signs of any external violence.

This concludes my list of cases, though it might easily be enlarged. Those given will suffice to indicate the method pursued.

I should like to add a few words with regard to one point in conducting an autopsy, and that is the method of opening the thorax. It is evident to me that not a few young practitioners, in common with the majority of students, sometimes experience great difficulties in this part of the examination, simply because they do not clearly appreciate the anatomical conditions.

In opening the wall of the thorax, the division of the cartilages should be made at a point as distant as possible from the sternum. As a matter of course, this direction applies only to non-ossified cartilages.

If, however, the cartilages are even only partially ossified, the bone-forceps must generally be substituted for the knife, and, under these circumstances, we may with advantage go farther outwards and divide the bones of the ribs in order to obtain free access to the viscera of the thorax. It may be observed that the sterno-clavicular joint is, as a rule, not ossified unless it has been the seat of severe disease. This joint is, therefore, always to be cut through ; and inasmuch as it is crescentic in form, and its surfaces are separated by an interarticular cartilage (see Fig. 4), separation is to be effected by means of steady strokes of the knife, directed in a crescentic curve round the sternal end of the clavicle.

The cartilage of the first rib, on the other hand, is very frequently ossified, even in cases where the other costal cartilages are free from bony deposit. As a rule, what we meet with here, as in the other costal cartilages, is a supra-cartilaginous, *i.e.*, a perichondrial ossification of great hardness, always enough to spoil the knife.

If there be no ossification, we first cut through the costal cartilages on each side close to their union with the ribs, the knife being held horizontally so that its point may not penetrate deeply into the thorax. The important point is to obtain as large an opening as possible into the thoracic cavity. The line of incision, therefore, describes on each side a curve, the convexity of which is towards the sternum, its lower end being continued for some distance in an outward direction, so as to strike the insertions of the cartilages of the last false ribs. A glance at Plate 4 will clearly show that from the second rib downwards the point of insertion of each successive rib becomes somewhat more distant from the mesial line. If these points are taken as a guide for the incisions, on removing the sternum and costal cartilages, we obtain a wide opening into the thorax, the width being much increased below.

The first rib, however, requires exceptional notice, for if the incision, as above described, be prolonged towards it, the knife will generally come against the bony *manubrium sterni*, which increases much in width at this part. Corresponding to the increase, the cartilage of the first rib extends much farther externally than that of the second, and the incision for its division must therefore be carried from one to two centimetres farther outward than that for

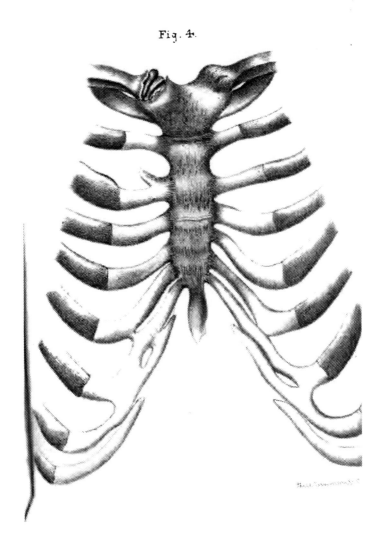

Fig. 4.

the second costal cartilage. The best way to proceed is to insert the knife, with its edge looking upwards and forwards, under the cartilage of the first rib, below its inferior border, and then cut upwards and forwards. This is the best way of avoiding injury to the vessels which are close beneath. Even in cases in which the perichondrial ossification is far advanced, the bony investing layers can often be readily cut through, if the knife is used in the above manner.

It is, therefore, always impossible to cut through the sterno-clavicular articulation and the first and second costal cartilages, by means of a single straight incision. Each of these parts must be divided separately and specially, and the knife must be directed in a suitable manner. Plate 4, which, moreover, shows partial duplication of the third costal cartilage on the right side, plainly illustrates the anatomical conditions, and any one who will carefully study it will be able, without difficulty, to draw the line by which the incisions are to be guided.

# REGULATIONS

### FOR THE

## GUIDANCE OF MEDICAL JURISTS

### IN CONDUCTING

## POST-MORTEM EXAMINATIONS FOR
## LEGAL PURPOSES.

### I. *General Directions.*

§ 1. *The Examining Medical Officers and their Duties.*——
The examination of a dead body for legal purposes is, in
accordance with the existing regulations, to be undertaken
by two medical practitioners only ; as a general rule, one of
these is to be a district-physician (Physicus, Gerichtsarzt),
and the other a district-surgeon (Gerichts-Kreis-Wundarzt).
A magistrate is to be present during the examination.

Those performing the examination are charged with the
duties of legal experts.

Should any doubts arise as to the method of performing
the examination, they are to be decided by the district-
physician or his substitute ; but the surgeon shall have the
right of expressing his dissentient view in the minutes of
proceedings.

§ 2. *Substitutes.*—Only when lawfully hindered from performing their functions may the above-mentioned medical
officers delegate their duties to substitutes. When possible,

physician who has passed the *pro physicatu* examination to be selected as a substitute.

§ 3. *Time of Performance.*—Autopsies should not, as a rule, take place until twenty-four hours after death; but the mere inspection of the dead body may be made earlier.

§ 4. *Course to be adopted when Putrefaction has set in.*— The presence of putrefaction is not, as a general rule, a sufficient reason for omitting the examination, and does not justify the medical jurist in refusing to proceed with his duties. For even if putrefaction be very far advanced, abnormalities and injuries of the bones can still be ascertained, and likewise many other circumstances, such as the colour and state of the hair, the absence of limbs, etc., which may assist in establishing the identity in doubtful cases. Foreign substances within the body may also be discovered, as also the presence or absence of pregnancy and of poisons. When, therefore, the question arises of disinterring a dead body for the purpose of gaining information on matters of this kind, it is the duty of the physicians to recommend the exhumation, regardless of the time that has elapsed since death took place.

§ 5. *Instruments.*—It is the duty of the medical jurists to take care that the following instruments, which are requisite for the performance of the examination, are forthcoming and in good order:—Four to six scalpels— two small, with a straight edge, and two large, with a curved edge. One razor. Two strong cartilage-knives. Two pairs of forceps. Two double hooks. Two pairs of scissors—one pair large, having one blade with the point rounded off, the other sharp; the other pair small, one blade probe-pointed, the other sharp-pointed. One pair of scissors for laying-open intestines. One blow-pipe furnished with a stopcock. One thick probe and two fine ones. One saw. A mallet and chisel. A pair of bone forceps. Six curved needles of various sizes. A pair of caliber compasses. A metre measure, divided into centimetres and millimetres. A measure graduated into divisions, showing 100, 50, and 25 cubic centimetres. A pair of scales, with weights up to 10 lbs. A good magnifying glass. Blue and red test-paper.

The cutting instruments must all be perfectly sharp. Physicians performing a post-mortem examination should, in addition, have at their command a microscope with two objectives, magnifying at least 400 diameters, as well as the various instruments required for making preparations; also glasses, reagents, etc.

§ 6. *Place for the Examination and Light.*—For the examination a sufficiently spacious and light room should be chosen, where the body can be placed in a suitable position, and in a quiet situation. It is not allowable to perform autopsies by artificial light, except in cases which admit of no delay. In such a case, the fact must be expressly alluded to in the protocol (§ 27), and mention made of the reason which rendered the performance at such a time imperative.

§ 7. *Frozen Bodies.*—If the body is frozen, it is to be brought into a warm room, and the examination is not to be proceeded with until the parts are sufficiently thawed. The employment of warm water, or other warm materials for expediting the thawing, is not allowable.

§ 8. *Transport of Dead Bodies.*—In moving the dead body in any way, and particularly in moving it from place to place, the greatest care must be taken to avoid applying any great pressure to any portion of it; and the large cavities should be kept as nearly as possible in a horizontal position.

II. *Proceedings at Post-mortem Examinations.*

§ 9. *The Judicial Objects of the Examination.*—Those charged with making the examination must keep their attention fixed upon the judicial objects in view, and all things which are subservient to these objects must be investigated with minuteness and completeness.

Everything that appears important, before being noted down in the minutes, must be shown to the magistrate.

§ 10. *Duties of the Examiners with Reference to the Investigation of any Peculiar Circumstances connected with the Case.*—Before commencing the examination, those charged with its performance should, whenever it appears necessary, request the magistrate for permission to inspect the place where the body was found, and ascertain the position which it occupied, and also to examine the clothes which were found on the deceased. As a general rule, however, they need not undertake these investigations, unless requested to do so by the magistrate.

They are also entitled to request the judgment of the magistrate with regard to all other circumstances, previously ascertained, which may be of importance for the examination, and the opinions to be formed thereupon.

§ 11. *Microscopical Examination.*—In all cases in which a microscopical examination is necessary in order to decide rapidly and positively as to any doubtful appearance—for example to distinguish blood from coloured fluids (holding hæmatin in solution)—such examination must be made while the autopsy is going on. When, owing to circumstances, this is impossible, or when it is necessary to make a difficult microscopical examination (*e.g.*, of portions of tissue) which cannot be done at once, the portions required are to be set aside in proper custody, and submitted to examination as soon as possible. In the report, the time at which this subsequent examination was made is to be definitely stated.

§ 12. *The Examination of the Body.*—The examination of the dead body consists of two principal parts :—

A. The external examination (inspection).
B. The internal examination (dissection).

§ 13. *External Examination.*—The external examinati͟ ͟ includes that of the external surface of the body in gener͟ and of its separate portions.

With reference to the condition of the body general͟ the following are the points to be ascertained and noted ͟—

1. Age ; sex ; size ; bodily conformation : general st͟ate of nutrition ; any signs of disease, such as ulcers about the legs, peculiar abnormalities, as spots, cicatrices, marks of tattooing, excess or deficiency of limbs.

2. The signs of death and of any decomposition which may be present.

Should the body be soiled with blood, fæces, dirt and the like, these must be washed off, and it must then be ascertained whether rigor mortis is present or not ; the colour of the skin generally must be noticed, and the kind and degree of any coloration or discoloration due to decomposition that may be present in any part, also the colour, position, and extent of the post-mortem stains, which must be cut into, examined, and carefully described, in order to discriminate between such appearances and those due to extravasation of blood.

With reference to individual portions of the body, the following points must be attended to :—

1. When the body is that of a person unknown, the colour and other peculiarities of the hair (of the head and the beard), and likewise the colour of the eyes are to be noted.

2. The presence of any foreign substances in the natural apertures of the body, the state of the teeth, and the condition and position of the tongue.

3. The following parts are then to be examined ;—the neck, chest, abdomen, back, the anus, the external organs of generation, and, lastly, the limbs.

Should there be an injury on any portion of the body, a *description* must be given of its shape, position, and direc-

:h reference to fixed points ; also its length and
in metric measurement. In this external exami-
iny probing of wounds and injuries is, as a general
be avoided, inasmuch as the depth can be readily
ied during the internal examination of the body
he injured parts. If those performing the autopsy
necessary to introduce a probe, they must do this
efully, and state their reasons for so doing in the
the proceedings (§ 27).

. wounds have been discovered, the condition of
rders and surrounding parts is to be determined,
r the examination and description of the wound in
nal state, it should be enlarged in order to ascertain
:nal condition of its borders and base.

. the body presents wounds and injuries which have
iothing to do with the cause of death—for example,
iade in attempts at rescue, bites of animals and the
 is sufficient that such appearances should be
ily noted.

*Internal Examination — General Directions.*—In
rnal examination, the three principal cavities of the
iz., the head, thorax, and abdomen are to be

pening of the vertebral canal, or of separate joints
 to be omitted in cases in which any information
expected from such examination.

i there is any definite suspicion with regard to the
f death, that cavity is first to be opened in which
cipal changes are supposed to exist; but in other
ie head is to be opened first, then the thorax, and,
he abdomen.*

:h of these cavities, the first thing to be done is to
ie the position of the organs therein contained ;
 colour and condition of their surfaces, the presence
ice of any unnatural contents, especially of foreign

With regard to new-born children, see Sections 23 and 24.

bodies, gases, fluids or coagula; and with regard to the two last substances, their quantity should be determined. Each separate organ is finally to be examined both externally and internally.

§ 15. *The Cavity of the Skull.*—Unless there are any injuries which have to be avoided by the knife, and which would necessitate some other method of procedure, the head is to be opened by means of an incision carried across the middle of the skull, from one ear to the other; the soft parts covering the head are then to be reflected backwards and forwards.

Attention having been paid to the condition of the soft parts, and of the surface of the bones, these latter are to be sawn through in a circular manner, and the skull-cap is to be removed. The cut surface, the internal surface, and the general condition of the cranial arch, are to be examined.

In the next place, the external surface of the dura mater is to be examined, the superior longitudinal sinus opened, and its contents determined; the dura mater is then to be divided on one side, and turned back, and its inner surface examined, as also the condition of the exposed portions of pia mater.

After this has been done on the other side, the brain is to be carefully removed, and the base of the skull is to be examined for any unusual contents. Attention must be paid to the condition of the dura and pia mater at the base and sides of the skull, and to that of the large arteries.

The transverse sinuses are next to be opened, and also the other sinuses (if there is any cause for so doing), and their contents are to be determined. The size and shape of the brain are next to be ascertained, and the colour, the fulness of the vessels, and the consistence and structure of the organ are to be determined by means of a series of incisions through individual portions, viz., the hemispheres of the cerebrum, the great ganglia (the optic thalamus and corpus striatum) the corpora quadrigemina, the cerebellum, the pons Varolii, and the medulla oblongata.

In addition to this, attention must always be paid to the condition of the tissue and vessels of the velum interpositum and choroid plexus.

The size and contents of the different ventricles, and likewise the condition and amount of fulness of the various venous plexuses, are to be carefully ascertained, and the presence or absence of any coagula external to the vessels is to be determined.

Finally, the bones of the base and lateral portions of the skull are to be examined, for which purpose the dura mater must be previously removed.

§ 16. *The Face, Parotid Gland, and Ear.*—When it is necessary to lay bare the internal parts of the face, and to examine the parotid gland or the ear, the incision carried over the head is to be prolonged behind the ears to the neck, and the skin is to be dissected forward, in order to spare it as much as possible. Particular attention is to be paid to the condition of the large arteries and veins.

§ 17. *The Vertebral Column and the Spinal Cord.*—The vertebral column (§ 14, par. 2) is to be opened from the posterior aspect. The skin and the subcutaneous fat are first to be divided exactly over the spinous processes; the muscles are then to be removed from the sides of these latter, and from the arches of the vertebræ. Extravasations of blood, lacerations and other injuries, particularly fractures of the bones, are to be carefully looked for.

Then by means of a chisel, or a vertebral saw if at hand, the spinous processes, together with the adjoining portions of the vertebral arches, are to be detached and removed. The dura mater is now exposed, and after its external surface has been examined, it is to be carefully slit open longitudinally, and the presence of any serum, or extravasated blood or other abnormal matters is to be determined. The colour, appearance, and general condition of the posterior portion of the pia mater are next to be noticed, and the resistance to pressure of the spinal cord is to be ascertained by gently passing the finger over it.

The roots of the nerves are next to be divided on both sides by a longitudinal incision; the lower end of the cord is to be carefully taken out, its anterior connections are next to be gradually separated, and, finally, the superior extremity is to be removed from the occipital foramen.

In carrying out these directions, great care must be taken that the spinal cord be neither pressed nor bent. When removed, the condition of the pia mater on the anterior aspect is first to be examined, then the size and colour (external) of the spinal cord are to be noted; and, lastly, numerous transverse incisions are to be made with a very sharp and thin knife, to determine the internal condition of the spinal cord, both of its white strands and of the grey substance. The dura mater is then to be removed from the bodies of the vertebræ, and the dissector is to examine for extravasation of blood, injuries or alterations in the bones or intervertebral cartilages.

§ 18. *Neck, Thorax, and Abdomen—General Directions.* —In opening the neck, thorax, and abdomen, it is generally sufficient to make one long incision from the chin to the pubes, passing to the left of the umbilicus. In ordinary cases, the incision is to be carried right into the abdominal cavity, care being taken not to injure any of its contents. The best plan is to make at first a very small incision into the peritoneum. Notice must be taken whether any gas or fluid escapes. First one, and then a second finger are introduced, the integuments are raised from the intestines, and the further incision through the peritoneum is to be made between the two fingers.

This being done, the position, colour, and other appearances presented by the exposed viscera, and also

the occurrence of any abnormal contents, are next to be
specified, and the position of the diaphragm is to be determined by examining it with the hand.

The examination of the abdominal organs is not to be
continued at this stage, unless there be particular reasons
for believing that the cause of death will be found in the
abdominal cavity (§ 14). As a general rule, the examination of the thorax must precede the further examination
of the abdomen.

§ 19. *The Thorax.*—For opening the thorax it is necessary that the soft parts of the chest should first be dissected
back beyond the points of attachment of the cartilages to
the ribs. The cartilages are then to be divided with a.
strong knife a few millimetres internal to their attachments. Care must be taken to avoid injuring the lung or
the heart. When the cartilages are ossified, the best plan
is to divide the ribs with a saw or bone-forceps a little
external to the attachments of the cartilages. The clavicles
are then to be separated from the manubrium of the
sternum by means of a crescentic incision, the knife being
held vertically, and the junction with the first rib,
whether cartilaginous or bony, is to be divided with the
knife or bone-forceps, the greatest care being taken to
avoid injuring the vessels lying beneath. Then the
attachments of the diaphragm, between the ends of the
two incisions, are to be divided close to the cartilages of
the false ribs and the ensiform cartilage ; the sternum is to
be turned upwards, and the mediastinum cut through, care
being taken to avoid injuring the pericardium and large
vessels.

After removing the sternum, the condition of the pleural
cavities is to be determined ; the presence, condition, and
quantity of any abnormal contents, the state of distension,
and the general appearance of the exposed portions of lung
are to be noticed. If, in the removal of the sternum, any
vessel has been injured, this must be tied, or a piece of

sponge must be applied to prevent the blood from escaping
into the pleural sac, where its presence might give rise to
mistakes. The condition of the mediastinum, the state of
the thymus gland, and likewise the condition of the large
vessels outside the pericardium (which vessels, however,
are not yet to be opened) are now to be noticed.

Then the pericardium is to be opened, and its condition
noticed, and the heart examined. With regard to the
latter, its size, the fulness of the coronary vessels, and of
its separate cavities (auricles and ventricles), its colour and
consistence (post-mortem rigidity) are all to be noticed
before any incision is made, and before the heart is removed
from the body. Then, while the heart is still unsevered from
its natural connections, each ventricle and each auricle are
to be separately opened, and the contents of each cavity are
to be determined with regard to their quantity, state of
coagulation and general appearance, and the size of the
auriculo-ventricular valves is to be tested by introducing
two fingers from the auricle. Then the heart is to be
removed ; the condition of the arterial openings is first to
be tested by pouring in water, and then, by slitting them
up ; the condition of the muscular tissue of the heart is to
be determined with reference to its colour and general
appearance. If there be reason to suppose that the
muscular structure has undergone considerable alteration
—fatty degeneration, for example—a microscopical examination must always be made.

The examination of the heart is to be followed by that
of the large vessels, but the descending aorta is to be left
until the lungs have been examined. In order to examine
the lungs minutely, they must be removed from the
thoracic cavity. Their removal must be effected with great
care, and the lung-tissue must not be torn or squeezed. If
extensive adhesions exist, and particularly if they are old-
standing, they must not be divided, but a portion of the
costal pleura should be removed with the attached adhesions.
After removal of the lungs, their surface is to be again

carefully examined, in order that recent changes—for example the commencement of inflammatory exudation—may not be overlooked. The capacity for air, the colour, and the consistence of each portion of the lungs, are to be noticed; finally, large smooth incisions are to be made, and the following points attended to:—The state of the cut surfaces; the amount of air, blood, and serum; the presence of any solid contents in the pulmonary vesicles; the condition of the bronchial tubes and pulmonary artery, with especial reference to obstruction, etc., in the latter. For this purpose, the air-passages and the large branches of the pulmonary artery are to be divided with the scissors, and followed out to their finer ramifications.

In cases where it is suspected that foreign matters have entered the air-passages, and where substances, the nature of which is not evident on simple inspection, are found in the air-tubes, recourse must be had to the microscope to determine their nature.

§ 20. *The Neck.*—According as circumstances may require, the neck may be examined either before or after the opening of the thorax or the removal of the lungs. Those performing the autopsy may, if they think fit, make a special examination of the larynx and air-tubes, if such investigation be of particular importance, as, for instance, in cases of death from strangulation or drowning.

As a general rule, the best plan is first to examine the large vessels and the nerve-trunks, and afterwards to open the larynx and trachea by an incision carried along their anterior aspect, and to examine their contents. In cases where it is especially important to examine these parts, they should be looked to before the lungs are removed from the body, and pressure should be carefully made upon these latter organs, in order to see whether any liquid matters, etc., ascend into the trachea.

The larynx is then to be removed, together with the

tongue, the soft palate, the pharynx, and the œsophag——
each of these parts is to be incised and its condition asc——
tained, the state of the mucous membrane being pa——
cularly noticed. The thyroid gland, the tonsils, ⌐
salivary glands, the cervical lymphatic glands, are all—
be examined.

In cases where the larynx or trachea has been injur——
or where important changes are supposed to exist in th—es
parts, an incision is not to be made into them until th—ey
have been removed from the body, and they are then to be
opened from their posterior aspect.

Where death has resulted from strangulation, or pre-
sumably from suffocation, and the carotid arteries are
opened in order to ascertain whether there is any injury
of the lining membrane, the vessels should be examined
while still in their natural position.

Finally, the state of the cervical vertebræ and of the
deep muscles of the neck should be noticed.

§ 21. *The Abdomen.*—In the further examination of the
abdominal cavity and of its contents (§ 18), a certain order
of sequence is always to be adopted, so that the removal
of an organ shall not interfere with the minute investigation of its relations to other parts. Thus the duodenum
and biliary ducts should be examined before the removal
of the liver. As a general rule, the following order of
sequence is advisable:—1. The omentum. 2. The spleen.
3. The kidneys and suprarenal capsules. 4. The urinary
bladder. 5. The organs of generation (in the male subject
the prostate gland and vesiculæ seminales, the testicles,
the penis, with the urethra; in the female, the ovaries,
Fallopian tubes, uterus, and vagina). 6. The rectum.
7. The duodenum and stomach. 8. The gall-ducts. 9.
The liver. 10. The pancreas. 11. The mesentery. 12.
The small intestines. 13. The large intestines. 14. The
large blood-vessels in front of the vertebral column; their
contents to be examined and determined.

*The Spleen.*—The length, breadth, and thickness of the spleen are to be ascertained while the organ is lying free, and not when placed in the hand, and the spleen is not to be compressed by the measure. A longitudinal incision is then to be made, and if any alterations of structure are manifest, the organ should be incised in various directions. The quantity of blood is always to be noticed.

*The Kidneys.*—Each kidney is to be removed by a vertical incision through the peritoneum, external to and behind the ascending or descending colon, the intestine is to be pushed aside, and the kidney detached from its connections. The capsule is then to be carefully removed, a long incision being made into it over the convex border of the kidney. The surface thus exposed is to be noticed with reference to the size, shape, colour, quantity of blood contained, and any morbid appearances that may be present. A long incision is then to be made through the kidney as far as its pelvis, the cut surface is to be washed with water, and described with reference to the condition of the cortical and medullary substance, vessels, and parenchyma.

*The Pelvic Organs.*—The organs of the pelvis (the bladder, rectum, and generative organs therewith connected) are best removed together, but the bladder should first be opened *in situ*, and its contents determined. Then the parts should be further examined, the generative organs being taken last. The vagina should be opened and examined before the uterus. In examining the body of a woman who has died after delivery, special attention should be paid to the condition of the veins and lymphatics, both on the inner surface of the uterus, and in its walls and appendages, the size and contents of the vessels being especially noted.

*The Stomach and Duodenum.*—The external condition of the stomach and duodenum is first to be ascertained while the parts are *in situ*. Then, with a pair of scissors, the duodenum is to be slit up on its anterior aspect, and the stomach along the great curvature ; the contents are then to be examined, the permeability of the gall duct and any matter contained therein are also to be noticed, and then the parts are to be removed for further examination.

*The Liver.*—The external appearance of the liver is first to be described, and the organ is to be removed after the examination of the excretory ducts. Long, smooth incisions are then to be carried transversely through the organ, and the amount of blood and general condition of the parenchyma are to be ascertained. The description is to contain a short account of the general condition of the lobules, the appearance of their centres and circumference being particularly noticed.

*The Small and Large Intestines.*—The small and large intestines are to be examined with reference to the degree of distension, colour, and other external appearances of their various parts ; they are then to be removed together, the mesentery being cut through close to the intestine. After removal, the intestine is to be slit up with the scissors along the line of attachment of the mesentery. As this is being done, the contents of each portion are to be noticed and estimated. Then the intestine is to be well cleansed with water, and the condition of the various portions noticed, particular attention being paid to the agminate and solitary glands, the villi, and valvulæ conniventes of the small intestine. In every case of peritoneal inflammation examine carefully the vermiform appendage.

§ 22. *Cases of Poisoning.*—In cases where poisoning is suspected, the abdominal cavity is first to be examined. Before anything further is done, attention is to be paid to the external appearance of the principal viscera, their position and size, the fulness of their vessels, and also as to whether there be any odour perceptible.

With regard to the vessels, the points here to be determined, as in other important organs, are as follows :—

Are the vessels arteries or veins? Does the congestion prevail in the finer ramifications, or only in the trunk and branches of a certain size? Are the intervascular spaces of considerable extent or not?

Double ligatures are then to be placed around the terminal portion of the œsophagus, just above the cardiac orifice, and two more around the duodenum, below the opening of the gall-duct. The parts are to be divided between the ligatures. The stomach is then to be removed with the duodenum, care being taken to avoid injuring the parts. They are then to be opened as described in § 21.

The contents are to be immediately examined with regard to the quantity, consistence, colour, composition, reaction, and smell, and placed in a clean porcelain or glass vessel.

The mucous membrane is then to be washed with water, and its colour, thickness, surface, and consistence are to be noticed. Particular attention is to be paid to the state of the blood-vessels, and to the tissue of the mucous membrane generally, and of each of the principal portions of the stomach. Particular care should be taken to ascertain whether any blood that may be present is within the vessels, or extravasated, also whether it is recent, or altered by putrefaction or digestion, and under these circumstances has penetrated by imbibition into the parts around. If extravasated, its situation should be determined—whether on the surface or in the tissue, and whether coagulated or not.

The surface of the mucous membrane is to be carefully examined for any breaches of continuity, such as loss of substance, erosions, or ulcers. The question as to whether the alterations manifested may have occurred after death, from natural decomposition, or from the action of the fermenting contents of the stomach, is to be carefully kept in mind.

This examination having been completed, the stomach and duodenum are to be placed in the vessel which contains

I 2

the contents (see above), and delivered to the magistrate for further investigation. The œsophagus having been tied in the neck and divided above the ligature, and subjected to examination, is also to be placed in the same vessel. In a case where the stomach contains but very little, the contents of the jejunum should be reserved in like manner.

Lastly, other materials and portions of organs, such as blood, urine, pieces of liver, kidneys, etc., are to be taken from the body, and made over to the magistrate separately for further examination. The urine is to be placed in a separate vessel. The blood is to be kept separately only in cases where a definite conclusion may be anticipated from spectrum-analysis. Portions of other organs reserved are to be placed together in one vessel.

Each vessel is to be carefully closed, sealed, and marked.

If on simple inspection the gastric mucous membrane appears particularly opaque and swollen, no time should be lost in examining it with the microscope, especial attention being paid to the condition of the peptic glands.

The microscope is also to be used in cases where the stomach contains any suspicious substances, such as portions of leaves or other vegetable matters, the remains of animal substances taken as food, etc.

Where trichinosis is suspected, the contents of the stomach and upper part of the jejunum are first to be subjected to microscopical examination, but portions of the muscular tissue (of the diaphragm, cervical and pectoral muscles) are to be put aside for further investigation.

§ 23. *New-born Children: Determination of Maturity and Period of Development.*—In the post-mortem examination of new-born children, special attention is to be directed to the following points in addition to the above-mentioned general rules :—

In the first place, the signs indicative of maturity and *period of* development must be looked for.

These are—the length and weight of the child, the condition of the general integuments and of the umbilical cord, the length and state of the hair of the head, the size of the fontanelles, the diameter of the cranium (longitudinal, transverse, and diagonal), the condition of the eyes (membrana pupillaris), the state of the cartilages of the nose and ear, the length and condition of the nails, the transverse diameter of the body at the shoulders and hips; in male infants, the condition of the scrotum and position of the testicles; in females, the condition of the external organs of generation.

Finally, we must examine the size of the centre of ossification (if present) in the inferior epiphysis of the femur. For this purpose, the knee-joint must be opened by means of a transverse incision below the patella, the joint fully bent and the patella removed; thin layers are then to be cut from the cartilaginous end of the femur, till the greatest transverse diameter of the centre of ossification (if present) be reached; this is to be measured in millimetres.

Should the condition of the fœtus be such as clearly to prove that it was born before the completion of the thirtieth week, it is not necessary to proceed further with the examination, unless the magistrate distinctly requires it.

§ 24. *Determination of the Question whether the Child has Breathed.*—If it shall appear that the child has been born after the thirtieth week, the next step is to ascertain whether it has breathed during or after birth. For this purpose the respiration-test must be applied, and the proceedings conducted in the following order:—

(a) Immediately on opening the abdominal cavity the position of the diaphragm is to be ascertained with reference to the corresponding rib, and on this account in new-born children the abdomen is always to be opened first, and afterwards the thorax and cranium.*

* The *dissection*, however, of the abdominal organs is never to precede the opening and examination of the thorax.

(*b*) Before opening the thorax a ligature is to be placed around the trachea above the sternum.

(*c*) The thorax is then to be opened, and attention must be paid to the degree of dilatation of the lungs, and their position dependent upon such dilatation, particularly with reference to the pericardium. The colour and consistence of the lungs should also be ascertained.

(*d*) The pericardium is then to be opened, and its condition and that of the heart externally are to be ascertained.

(*e*) The cavities of the heart are then to be opened, and their contents to be examined, and the condition of the heart in other respects is to be determined.

(*f*) The larynx and the portion of the trachea above the ligature are then to be opened by means of a longitudinal incision, the condition of their walls is to be ascertained, and any contents are to be examined.

(*g*) The trachea is to be divided above the ligature and removed, together with all the organs of the thorax.

(*h*) After removing the thymus gland and the heart, the lungs are to be placed in a capacious vessel filled with clean cold water, in order to test their buoyancy.

(*i*) The lower part of the trachea and its subdivisions are to be laid open and examined, especially with reference to their contents.

(*k*) Incisions are to be made in both lungs, and notice taken whether any crepitating sound be heard, and also with reference to the amount and quality of the blood issuing from these cut surfaces on slight pressure.

(*l*) Incisions are to be made into the lungs below the surface of the water, in order to see whether any air-bubbles rise from the cut surfaces.

(*m*) Both lungs are next to be separated into their lobes,

and these are to be divided into several small pieces, the buoyancy of each of which is to be tested.

(*n*) The œsophagus is to be opened and its condition ascertained.

(*o*) Lastly, in cases where it is suspected that air cannot gain access to the lungs in consequence of the filling up of their cells and passages with morbid products (hepatisation) or foreign substances (mucus, meconium), the lung-tissue is to be examined with the microscope.

§ 25. *Other Examinations.*—In the last place, it is the duty of those performing the autopsy to examine all other organs or parts not mentioned by name in the regulations, in any case in which the parts in question are found to be injured or otherwise abnormal.

§ 26. *End of the Examination—The Cavities to be Closed.*—The examination being completed and the body cleansed as far as possible, it is the duty of the district-surgeon, who is relatively the junior of the medical examiners, to close up carefully those cavities of the body which have been opened.

III. *Framing the Protocol and Report of the Examination.*

§ 27. *Drawing up of the Protocol of the Examination.*—A protocol of everything connected with the post-mortem examination must be drawn up by the magistrate upon the spot.

The physician (Gerichtsarzt) has to take care that the appearances in all details, as determined upon by the inspectors, are literally described in the protocol.

The magistrate is to direct that this should be done in such a way that the description and the report of each separate organ are to be placed on record before another portion is submitted to examination.

§ 28. *Arrangement and Drawing up of the Protocol.*—— The technical portion of the protocol of the autopsy must be dictated by the physician; it must be clear, definite, and intelligible to non-medical persons. And for this latter purpose, especially in the description of the appearances found, the use of foreign scientific terms is to be avoided, when this can be done without loss of distinctness.

The two principal divisions—the external and internal inspections—are to be distinguished by large capitals (A & B); the sections describing the opening of the cavities, in the order in which this has been done, by Roman numerals (I., II.). The opening of the thoracic and abdominal cavities will come under one number. In the section which deals with the thorax and abdomen, the general appearances, mentioned in the last paragraph of Section 18, are first to be described, then under *a* and *b* the appearance of the thoracic and abdominal organs respectively.

The result of the examination of each separate part is to be contained in a distinct paragraph headed with Arabic numerals. The numerals run consecutively from the beginning to the end of the protocol.

The appearances found must be accurately described as matters of fact and not in the form of mere opinions (*e.g.*, "inflamed," "gangrenous," "healthy," "normal," "a wound," "an ulcer," and the like). But the inspectors may, if they please, for the sake of distinctness, add to their statement of actual observations expressions of this kind in parenthesis.

In all cases a statement must be given with reference to the amount of blood contained in each important part, and what is required is a terse description, not merely an opinion couched in such terms as "intensely," "moderately," "somewhat," or "very reddened," "full of blood," "bloodless." In the description, the size, shape, colour, and consistence of the various parts are to be mentioned *seriatim* before making any incisions.

§ 29. *Provisional Opinion.*—At the conclusion of the

autopsy, the medical inspectors must enter in the protocol their provisional opinion regarding the case summarily and without the addition of any reasons.

If any particular facts influencing their opinion have come to their knowledge, whether from the proceedings or otherwise, these must be briefly mentioned.

If any particular questions have been put to them by the magistrate, it must be shown in the protocol that the answer is the result of such questions.

In every case the cause of death as evidenced by the objective appearances is first to be set forth in the opinion, and next the question of criminality is to be dealt with.

If the cause of death has not been discovered, the fact must be expressly mentioned. It is never sufficient to say that the death has resulted from internal causes or from disease; the disease must be specified.

In cases where further technical examination is necessary, or where there are any doubtful circumstances, a special opinion giving reasons is to be formally deferred.

§ 30. *Supplementary Explanation with regard to Weapons.* —If there be any injuries on the dead body which may have been the cause of death, and if it be suspected that a weapon found has been used to cause the injuries, then the medical inspectors, at the request of the magistrate, must institute a comparison between them, and must state whether and what injuries could have been caused by the weapon, and whether any conclusions can be drawn from the position and condition of the injury, as to the mode in which the perpetrator has acted, and as to the force used.

Should weapons not be forthcoming, the inspectors must express an opinion, as far as the appearances will permit, with regard to the way in which the injuries have originated, and with reference to the nature of the weapon employed.

§ 31. *Report of the Examination.*—Should a report (a reasoned opinion) of the examination be required from the inspectors, it is to be furnished in the following form:—

All useless formalities being avoided, and after a statement of what has been done, it is to be commenced with a condensed but minute history of the case, so far as their cognizance permits. They must then incorporate in this report the protocol of the autopsy, but only so much as is necessary for the elucidation of the case, using the exact words of the protocol and the same numerals, expressly drawing attention to any deviations in this respect.

The style of the report must be concise and clear, and the ground on which the opinion is formed must be displayed in such a way as to be intelligible and convincing even to non-medical men. The inspectors must employ, therefore, as far as possible, expressions and terms in popular use. Especial references to literary authorities are, as a rule, to be avoided.

If the magistrate has placed definite questions before the inspectors for their opinion, these must be answered as fully and literally as possible, or the reasons given why this cannot be done.

The report of the examination must be signed by both inspectors, and if a district-physician has assisted at the autopsy, his official seal must be affixed to the report.

Every report, when required, must be furnished by the inspectors within four weeks at latest.

BERLIN, *January* 6, 1875.

*The Royal Scientific Commission for Medical Affairs.*

The foregoing regulations are hereby approved, and their observance is rendered obligatory upon all medical officers who may be concerned. The regulations of the 15th of November, 1858, are abolished.

BERLIN, *February* 13, 1875.

*The Minister for Ecclesiastical, Educational, and Medical Affairs.*

FALK.

London: Pardon and Sons, Printers, Paternoster Row.

LONDON, *November*, 1879.

# J. & A. CHURCHILL'S

# MEDICAL CLASS BOOKS.

## ANATOMY.

*RAUNE.*—An Atlas of Topographical Anatomy, after Plane Sections of Frozen Bodies. By WILHELM BRAUNE, Professor of Anatomy in the University of Leipsig. Translated by EDWARD BELLAMY, F.R.C.S., Surgeon to Charing-Cross Hospital, and Lecturer on Anatomy in its School. With 34 Photo-lithographic Plates and 48 Woodcuts. Large imp. 8vo, 40s.

*LOWER.*—Diagrams of the Nerves of the Human Body, exhibiting their Origin, Divisions, and Connexions, with their Distribution to the various Regions of the Cutaneous Surface, and to all the Muscles. By WILLIAM H. FLOWER, F.R.C.S., F.R.S., Conservator of the Museum of the Royal College of Surgeons. Second Edition, containing 6 Plates. Royal 4to, 12s.

*ODLEE.*—An Atlas of Human Anatomy: illustrating most of the ordinary Dissections; and many not usually practised by the Student. By RICKMAN J. GODLEE, M.S., F.R.C.S., Assistant-Surgeon to University College Hospital, and Senior Demonstrator of Anatomy in University College. To be completed in 12 or 13 Bi-monthly Parts, each containing 4 Coloured Plates, with Explanatory Text. Parts I to X. Imp. 4to, 7s. 6d. each.

*EATH.*—Practical Anatomy: a Manual of Dissections. By CHRISTOPHER HEATH, F.R.C.S., Holme Professor of Clinical Surgery in University College and Surgeon to the Hospital. Fourth Edition. With 16 Coloured Plates and 264 Engravings. Crown 8vo, 14s.

---

*NEW BURLINGTON STREET.*

## ANATOMY—*continued.*

*HOLDEN.*—Human Osteology : comprising a
Description of the Bones. with Delineations of the Attachments of the
Muscles, the General and Microscopical Structure of Bone and its
Development. By LUTHER HOLDEN, F.R.C.S., Senior Surgeon to St.
Bartholomew's and the Foundling Hospitals, and ALBAN DORAN,
F.R.C.S., late Anatomical, now Pathological, Assistant to the Museum
of the Royal College of Surgeons. Fifth Edition. With 61 Lithographic
Plates and 89 Engravings. Royal 8vo, 15s.

*By the same Author.*

A Manual of the Dissection of the
Human Body. Fourth Edition. Revised by the Author and
JOHN LANGTON, F.R.C.S., Assistant Surgeon and Lecturer on
Anatomy at St. Bartholomew's Hospital. With Engravings.
8vo, 16s.

ALSO,

Landmarks, Medical and Surgical. Second
Edition. 8vo, 3s. 6d.

*MORRIS.*—The Anatomy of the Joints of Man.
By HENRY MORRIS, M.A., F.R.C.S., Surgeon to, and Lecturer on Ana-
tomy and Practical Surgery at, the Middlesex Hospital. With
Plates (19 Coloured) and Engravings. 8vo, 16s.

*WAGSTAFFE.*—The Student's Guide to Human
Osteology. By WM. WARWICK WAGSTAFFE, F.R.C.S., Assistant-
Surgeon to, and Lecturer on Anatomy at, St. Thomas's Hospital.
With 23 Plates and 66 Engravings. Fcap. 8vo, 10s. 6d.

*WILSON.*—The Anatomist's Vade-Mecum: a
System of Human Anatomy. By ERASMUS WILSON, F.R.C.S., F.R.S.,
late Professor of Dermatology to the Royal College of Surgeons.
Ninth Edition, by G. BUCHANAN, M.A., M.D., late Professor of Clinical
Surgery in the University of Glasgow, and HENRY E. CLARK, F.F.P.S.,
Lecturer on Anatomy in the Glasgow Royal Infirmary School of
Medicine. With 371 Engravings. Crown 8vo, 14s.

Anatomical Remembrancer (the) ; or, Complete Pocket Anatomist. Eighth Edition. 32mo, 3s. 6d.

## BOTANY.

*ENTLEY.*—A Manual of Botany. By Robert
BENTLEY, F.L.S., Professor of Botany in King's College and to the
Pharmaceutical ' Society. With 1138 Engravings. Third Edition.
Crown 8vo, 14s.

*ENTLEY AND TRIMEN.*—Medicinal Plants:
being descriptions, with original Figures, of the Principal Plants
employed in Medicine, and an account of their Properties and Uses
By ROBERT BENTLEY, F.L.S., and HENRY TRIMEN, M.B., F.L.S., British
Museum, and Lecturer on Botany at St. Mary's Hospital Medical
School. To be completed in 42 Monthly Parts, each containing 8
Coloured Plates. Parts I. to XL. Large 8vo, 5s. each part.

## CHEMISTRY.

*ERNAYS.*—Notes for Students in Chemistry;
being a Syllabus of Chemistry compiled mainly from the Manuals of
Fownes-Watts, Miller, Wurz, and Schorlemmer. By ALBERT J. BERNAYS,
Ph.D., Professor of Chemistry at St. Thomas's Hospital, Examiner
in Chemistry at the Royal College of Physicians of London. Sixth
Edition. Fcap. 8vo, 3s. 6d.

*By the same Author.*

Skeleton Notes on Analytical Chemistry,
for Students in Medicine. Fcap. 8vo, 2s. 6d.

*LOXAM.*—Chemistry, Inorganic and Organic;
with Experiments. By CHARLES L. BLOXAM, Professor of Chemistry in
King's College. Third Edition. With 295 Engravings. 8vo, 16s.

*By the same Author.*

Laboratory Teaching; or, Progressive
Exercises in Practical Chemistry. Fourth Edition. With 83
Engravings. Crown 8vo, 5s. 6d.

*OWMAN AND BLOXAM.*—Practical Chemistry,
including Analysis. By JOHN E. BOWMAN, Formerly Professor of
Practical Chemistry in King's College, and CHARLES L. BLOXAM,
Professor of Chemistry in King's College. With 93 Engravings.
Seventh Edition. Fcap. 8vo, 6s. 6d.

## CHEMISTRY—*continued.*

**CLOWES.**—Practical Chemistry and Qualitative Inorganic Analysis. An Elementary Treatise specially adapted for use in the Laboratories of Schools and Colleges, and by Beginners. By FRANK CLOWES, D.SC., Senior Science Master at the High School, Newcastle-under-Lyme. Second Edition. With 47 Engravings. Post 8vo, 7s. 6d.

**FOWNES AND WATTS.**—Physical and Inorganic Chemistry. Twelfth Edition. By GEORGE FOWNES, F.R.S., and HENRY WATTS, B.A., F.R.S. With 154 Engravings, and Coloured Plate of Spectra. Crown 8vo, 8s. 6d.

*By the same Authors.*

Chemistry of Carbon - Compounds, or Organic Chemistry. Twelfth Edition. With Engravings. Crown 8vo, 10s.

**GALLOWAY.**—A Manual of Qualitative Analysis. By ROBERT GALLOWAY, Professor of Applied Chemistry in the Royal College of Science for Ireland. Fifth Edition. With Engravings. Post 8vo, 8s. 6d.

**VACHER.**—A Primer of Chemistry, including Analysis. By ARTHUR VACHER. 18mo, 1s.

**VALENTIN.**—Introduction to Inorganic Chemistry. By WILLIAM G. VALENTIN, F.C.S., Late Principal Demonstrator of Practical Chemistry in the Science Training Schools. Third Edition. With 82 Engravings. 8vo, 6s. 6d.

*By the same Author.*

A Course of Qualitative Chemical Analysis. Fourth Edition. With 19 Engravings. 8vo, 7s. 6d.

ALSO,

Chemical Tables for the Lecture-room and Laboratory. In Five large Sheets, 5s. 6d.

### CHILDREN, DISEASES OF.

*ELLIS.*—A Practical Manual of the Diseases
of Children. By EDWARD ELLIS, M.D., late Senior Physician to the
Victoria Hospital for Sick Children. With a Formulary. Third
Edition. Crown 8vo, 7s. 6d.

*SMITH.* — Clinical Studies of Disease in
Children. By EUSTACE SMITH, M.D., F.R.C.P., Physician to H.M. the
King of the Belgians, and to the East London Hospital for Children.
Post 8vo, 7s. 6d.

*By the same Author.*

On the Wasting Diseases of Infants and
Children. Third Edition. Post 8vo, 8s. 6d.

*STEINER.*—Compendium of Children's Dis-
eases; a Handbook for Practitioners and Students. By JOHANN
STEINER, M.D. Translated from the Second German Edition, by LAWSON
TAIT, F.R.C.S., Surgeon to the Birmingham Hospital for Women, &c.
8vo, 12s. 6d.

### DENTISTRY.

*SEWILL.*—The Student's Guide to Dental
Anatomy and Surgery. By HENRY E. SEWILL, M.R.C.S., L.D.S., late
Dental Surgeon to the West London Hospital. With 77 Engravings.
Fcap. 8vo, 5s. 6d.

*SMITH.*—Handbook of Dental Anatomy and
Surgery. For the Use of Students and Practitioners. By JOHN SMITH,
M.D., F.R.S.E., Dental Surgeon to the Royal Infirmary, Edinburgh.
Second Edition. Fcap. 8vo, 4s. 6d.

*STOCKEN.*—Elements of Dental Materia Medica
and Therapeutics, with Pharmacopœia. By JAMES STOCKEN, L.D.S.R.C.S.,
Lecturer on Dental Materia Medica and Therapeutics and Dental
Surgeon to the National Dental Hospital. Second Edition. Fcap. 8vo,
6s. 6d.

## DENTISTRY—*continued*.

*TAFT.*—A Practical Treatise on Operative
Dentistry. By JONATHAN TAFT, D.D.S., Professor of Operative Surgery
in the Ohio College of Dental Surgery. Third Edition. With 134
Engravings. 8vo, 18s.

*TOMES (C. S.).*—Manual of Dental Anatomy,
Human and Comparative. By CHARLES S. TOMES, M.A., M.R.C.S.,
Lecturer on Anatomy and Physiology at the Dental Hospital of London.
With 179 Engravings. Crown 8vo, 10s. 6d.

*TOMES (J. and C. S.).*—A Manual of Dental
Surgery. By JOHN TOMES, M.R.C.S., F.R.S., Consulting Surgeon-Dentist
to Middlesex Hospital; and CHARLES S. TOMES, M.A., M.R.C.S.,
Lecturer on Anatomy and Physiology at the Dental Hospital of London. Second Edition. With 262 Engravings. Fcap. 8vo, 14s.

## EAR, DISEASES OF.

*BURNETT.*—The Ear: its Anatomy, Physio-
logy, and Diseases. A Practical Treatise for the Use of Medical
Students and Practitioners. By CHARLES H. BURNETT, M.D., Aural
Surgeon to the Presbyterian Hospital, Philadelphia. With 87 Engravings. 8vo, 18s.

*DALBY.*—On Diseases and Injuries of the Ear.
By WILLIAM B. DALBY, F.R.C.S., Aural Surgeon to, and Lecturer on
Aural Surgery at, St. George's Hospital. With Engravings. Fcap. 8vo,
6s. 6d.

*JONES.*—A Practical Treatise on Aural Sur-
gery. By H. MACNAUGHTON JONES, M.D., Professor of the Queen's
University in Ireland, Surgeon to the Cork Ophthalmic and Aural Hospital. With 46 Engravings. Crown 8vo, 5s.

*By the same Author.*

Atlas of the Diseases of the Membrana
Tympani. In Coloured Plates, containing 59 Figures. With Explanatory Text. Crown 4to, 21s.

## FORENSIC MEDICINE.

*OGSTON.*—Lectures on Medical Jurisprudence.
By Francis Ogston, M.D., Professor of Medical Jurisprudence and Medical Logic in the University of Aberdeen. Edited by Francis Ogston, Jun., M.D., Assistant to the Professor of Medical Jurisprudence and Lecturer on Practical Toxicology in the University of Aberdeen. With 12 Plates. 8vo, 18s.

*TAYLOR.*—The Principles and Practice of Medical Jurisprudence. By Alfred S. Taylor, M.D., F.R.S., Professor of Medical Jurisprudence to Guy's Hospital. Second Edition. With 189 Engravings. 2 Vols. 8vo, 31s. 6d.

*By the same Author.*

A Manual of Medical Jurisprudence.
Tenth Edition. With 55 Engravings. Crown 8vo, 14s.

ALSO,

Oı Poisons, in relation to Medical Juris-
.prudence and Medicine. Third Edition. With 104 Engravings. Crown 8vo, 16s.

*WOOIMAN AND TIDY.*—A Handy-Book of Forensic Medicine and Toxicology. By W. Bathurst Woodman, M.D., F.R.P.; and C. Meymott Tidy, M.B., Professor of Chemistry and of Medical Jurisprudence, &c., at the London Hospital. With 8 Lithographic Plates and 116 Wood Engravings. 8vo, 31s. 6d.

---

## HYGIENE.

*WILSN.*—A Handbook of Hygiene and Sanitar Science. By George Wilson, M.A., M.D., Medical Officer of Health for Mid Warwickshire. Fourth Edition. With Engravings. Po8vo, 10s. 6d.

---

*NEW BURLINGTON* STREET.

## HYGIENE—*continued.*

*PARKES.*—A Manual of Practical Hygiene.
By EDMUND A. PARKES, M.D., F.R.S. Fifth Edition by F. DE CHAUMONT,
M.D., F.R.S., Professor of Military Hygiene in the Army Medical
School. With 9 Plates and 112 Engravings. 8vo, 18s.

*By the same Author.*

Public Health: being a Concise Sketch of
the Sanitary Considerations connected with the Land, with Cities,
Villages, Houses, and Individuals. Revised by WILLIAM AITKEN,
M.D., F.R.S., Professor of Pathology in the Army Medical
School. Crown 8vo, 2s. 6d.

---

## MATERIA MEDICA AND THERAPEUTICS.

*BINZ AND SPARKS.*—The Elements of Therapeutics: a Clinical Guide to the Action of Medicine. By C.
BINZ, M.D., Professor of Pharmacology in the University of Bonn.
Translated from the Fifth German Edition, and Edited with additions,
in conformity with the British and American Pharmacopœias, by
EDWARD I. SPARKS, M.A., M.B. Oxon., F.R.C.P. Lond. Crown 8vo,
8s. 6d.

*ROYLE AND HARLEY.*—A Manual of Materia
Medica and Therapeutics. By J. FORBES ROYLE, M.D., F.S., for-
merly Professor of Materia Medica in King's College; and JOHN
HARLEY, M.D., F.R.C.P., Physician to, and Joint Lecturer : Clinical
Medicine at, St. Thomas's Hospital. Sixth Edition. With 1: Engrav-
ings. Crown 8vo, 15s.

*THOROWGOOD.*—The Student's Guide to
Materia Medica. By JOHN C. THOROWGOOD, M.D., F.R.C.P. Lecturer
on Materia Medica at the Middlesex Hospital. With Engravings.
Fcap. 8vo, 6s. 6d.

*WARING.*—A Manual of Practical Therapeu-
tics. By EDWARD J. WARING, M.D., F.R.C.P., Retired Surgn H.M.
Indian Army. Third Edition. Fcap. 8vo, 12s. 6d.

---

## MEDICINE.

*ARCLAY.*—**A Manual of Medical Diagnosis.**
By A. WHYTE BARCLAY, M.D., F.R.C.P., Physician to, and Lecturer on
Medicine at, St. George's Hospital. Third Edition. Fcap. 8vo, 10s. 6d.

*ARLOW.*—**A Manual of the Practice of**
Medicine. By HILARO BARLOW, M.D., Formerly Senior Physician to
Guy's Hospital. Second Edition. Fcap. 8vo, 7s. 6d.

*HARTERIS.*—**The Student's Guide to the**
Practice of Medicine. By MATTHEW CHARTERIS, M.D., Professor of
Practice of Medicine, Anderson's College; Physician and Lecturer on
Clinical Medicine, Royal Infirmary, Glasgow. With Engravings on
Copper and Wood. Second Edition. Fcap. 8vo, 6s. 6d.

*ENWICK.*—**The Student's Guide to Medical**
Diagnosis. By SAMUEL FENWICK, M.D., F.R.C.P., Physician to the
London Hospital. Fourth Edition. With 106 Engravings. Fcap. 8vo,
6s. 6d.

*By the same Author.*

**The Student's Outlines of Medical Treat-**
ment. Fcap. 8vo., 7s.

*LINT.*—**Clinical Medicine : a Systematic Trea-**
tise on the Diagnosis and Treatment of Disease. By AUSTIN FLINT,
M.D., Professor of the Principles and Practice of Medicine, &c., in
Bellevue Hospital Medical College. 8vo, 20s.

*By the same Author.*

**A Manual of Percussion and Auscultation ;**
of the Physical Diagnosis of Diseases of the Lungs and Heart, and
of Thoracic Aneurism. Post 8vo, 6s. 6d.

*ALL.*—**Synopsis of the Diseases of the Larynx,**
Lungs, and Heart : comprising Dr. Edwards' Tables on the Examina-
tion of the Chest. With Alterations and Additions. By F. DE
HAVILLAND HALL, M.D., Assistant-Physician to the Westminster
Hospital. Royal 8vo, 2s. 6d.

## MIDWIFERY.

*BARNES.*—Lectures on Obstetric Operations,
including the Treatment of Hæmorrhage, and forming a Guide to the
Management of Difficult Labour. By ROBERT BARNES, M.D., F.R.C.P.,
Obstetric Physician to, and Lecturer on Diseases of Women, &c., at St.
George's Hospital. Third Edition. With 124 Engravings. 8vo, 18s.

*CLAY.*—The Complete Handbook of Obstetric
Surgery; or, Short Rules of Practice in every Emergency, from the
Simplest to the most formidable Operations connected with the Science
of Obstetricy. By CHARLES CLAY, M.D., late Senior Surgeon to, and
Lecturer on Midwifery at, St. Mary's Hospital, Manchester. Third
Edition. With 91 Engravings. Fcap. 8vo, 6s. 6d.

*RAMSBOTHAM.*—The Principles and Practice
of Obstetric Medicine and Surgery. By FRANCIS H. RAMSBOTHAM, M.D.,
formerly Obstetric Physician to the London Hospital. Fifth Edition.
Illustrated with 120 Plates, forming one thick handsome volume. 8vo,
22s.

*ROBERTS.*—The Student's Guide to the Practice
of Midwifery. By D. LLOYD ROBERTS, M.D., F.R.C.P., Physician to
St. Mary's Hospital, Manchester. Second Edition. With 96 Engravings. Fcap. 8vo, 7s.

*SCHROEDER.*—A Manual of Midwifery; includ-
ing the Pathology of Pregnancy and the Puerperal State. By KARL
SCHROEDER, M.D., Professor of Midwifery in the University of Erlangen.
Translated by CHARLES H. CARTER, M.D. With Engravings. 8vo,
12s. 6d.

*SWAYNE.*—Obstetric Aphorisms for the Use of
Students commencing Midwifery Practice. By JOSEPH G. SWAYNE,
M.D., Lecturer on Midwifery at the Bristol School of Medicine. Sixth
Edition. With Engravings. Fcap. 8vo, 3s. 6d.

# MICROSCOPY.

*CARPENTER.*—The Microscope and its Revela-
tions. By WILLIAM B. CARPENTER, C.B., M.D., F.R.S., late Registrar
to the University of London. Fifth Edition. With more than 500
Engravings. Crown 8vo, 15s.

*MARSH.*—Section-Cutting: a Practical Guide
to the Preparation and Mounting of Sections for the Microscope, special
prominence being given to the subject of Animal Sections. By Dr.
SYLVESTER MARSH. With Engravings. Fcap. 8vo, 2s. 6d.

*MARTIN.*—A Manual of Microscopic Mounting.
By JOHN H. MARTIN, Member of the Society of Public Analysts, &c.
Second Edition. With several Plates and 144 Engravings. 8vo, 7s. 6d.

*WYTHE.*—The Microscopist: a Manual of
Microscopy and Compendium of the Microscopic Sciences, Micro-
Mineralogy, Micro-Chemistry, Biology, Histology, and Pathological
Histology. By J. H. WYTHE, A.M., M.D., Professor of Microscopy and
Biology in the San Francisco Medical College. Third Edition. With
205 Illustrations. Royal 8vo, 18s.

# OPHTHALMOLOGY.

*HIGGENS.*—Hints on Ophthalmic Out-Patient
Practice. By CHARLES HIGGENS, F.R.C.S., Ophthalmic Assistant-Sur-
geon to, and Lecturer on Ophthalmology at, Guy's Hospital. Second
Edition. Fcap. 8vo, 2s.

*JONES.*—A Manual of the Principles and
Practice of Ophthalmic Medicine and Surgery. By T. WHARTON JONES,
F.R.C.S., F.R.S., Ophthalmic Surgeon and Professor of Ophthalmology
to University College Hospital. Third Edition. With 9 Coloured
Plates and 173 Engravings. Fcap. 8vo, 12s. 6d.

*MACNAMARA.*—A Manual of the Diseases of
the Eye. By CHARLES MACNAMARA, F.R.C.S., Surgeon to Westminster
Hospital. Third Edition. With 7 Coloured Plates and 52 Engravings.
Fcap. 8vo, 12s. 6d.

## OPHTHALMOLOGY—*continued.*

*NETTLESHIP.*—The Student's Guide to Diseases
of the Eye. By EDWARD NETTLESHIP, F.R.C.S., Ophthalmic Surgeon
to, and Lecturer on Ophthalmic Surgery at, St. Thomas's Hospital.
With 48 Engravings. Fcap. 8vo, 7s. 6d.

*WELLS.* —A Treatise on the Diseases of the
Eye. By J. SOELBERG WELLS, F.R.C.S., Ophthalmic Surgeon to King's
College Hospital, Professor of Ophthalmology at King's College. With
Coloured Plates and Engravings. Third Edition. 8vo, 25s.

---

## PATHOLOGY.

*JONES AND SIEVEKING.*—A Manual of Patho-
logical Anatomy. By C. HANDFIELD JONES, M.B., F.R.S., Physician to
St. Mary's Hospital, and EDWARD H. SIEVEKING, M.D., F.R.C.P., Physi-
cian to St. Mary's Hospital. Second Edition. Edited by J. F. PAYNE,
M.B., Assistant-Physician and Lecturer on General Pathology at St.
Thomas's Hospital. With 195 Engravings. Crown 8vo, 16s.

*VIRCHOW.* — Post-Mortem Examinations: a
Description and Explanation of the Method of Performing them,
with especial reference to Medico-Legal Practice. By Professor
RUDOLPH VIRCHOW, Berlin Charité Hospital. Fcap. 8vo, 2s. 6d.

*WILKS AND MOXON.*—Lectures on Pathologi-
cal Anatomy. By SAMUEL WILKS, M.D., F.R.S., Physician to, and
Lecturer on Medicine at, Guy's Hospital; and WALTER MOXON, M.D.,
F.R.C.P., Physician to, and Lecturer on Clinical Medicine at, Guy's
Hospital. Second Edition. With 5 Steel Plates. 8vo, 18s.

---

## PSYCHOLOGY.

*BUCKNILL AND TUKE.*—A Manual of Psycho-
logical Medicine: containing the Lunacy Laws, Nosology, Ætiology,
Statistics, Description, Diagnosis, Pathology, and Treatment of Insanity,
with an Appendix of Cases. By JOHN C. BUCKNILL, M.D., F.R.S.,
and D. HACK TUKE, M.D., F.R.C.P. Fourth Edition, with 12 Plates
(30 Figures). 8vo, 25s.

---

## PHYSIOLOGY.

*CARPENTER.*—Principles of Human Physio-
logy. With 3 Steel Plates and 371 Engravings. By WILLIAM B.
CARPENTER, C.B., M.D., F.R.S., late Registrar to the University of
London. Eighth Edition. Edited by Mr. Henry Power. 8vo, 31s. 6d.

*By the same Author.*

A Manual of Physiology. With upwards
of 250 Illustrations. Fifth Edition. Edited by P. H. PYE-SMITH,
M.D., F.R.C.P. Crown 8vo. [*In the press.*

*DALTON.*—A Treatise on Human Physiology :
designed for the use of Students and Practitioners of Medicine. By
JOHN C. DALTON, M.D., Professor of Physiology and Hygiene in the
College of Physicians and Surgeons, New York. Sixth Edition. With
316 Engravings. Royal 8vo, 20s.

*FREY.*—The Histology and Histo-Chemistry of
Man. A Treatise on the Elements of Composition and Structure of the
Human Body. By HEINRICH FREY, Professor of Medicine in Zurich.
Translated from the Fourth German Edition, by ARTHUR E. BARKER,
Assistant-Surgeon to the University College Hospital. With 608
Engravings. 8vo, 21s.

*RUTHERFORD.*—Outlines of Practical Histo-
logy. By WILLIAM RUTHERFORD, M.D., F.R.S., Professor of the Insti-
tutes of Medicine in the University of Edinburgh ; Examiner in
Physiology in the University of London. Second Edition. With 63
Engravings. Crown 8vo (with additional leaves for Notes), 6s.

*SANDERSON.*—Handbook for the Physiological
Laboratory : containing an Exposition of the fundamental facts of the
Science, with explicit Directions for their demonstration. By J. BURDON
SANDERSON, M.D., F.R.S., Professor and Superintendent of the Brown
Institution ; E. KLEIN, M.D., F.R.S., Assistant-Professor in the Brown
Institution ; MICHAEL FOSTER, M.D., F.R.S., Prælector of Physiology
at Trinity College, Cambridge ; and T. LAUDER BRUNTON, M.D., F.R.S.,
Lecturer on Materia Medica at St. Bartholomew's Hospital Medical
College. 2 Vols., with 123 Plates. 8vo, 24s.

## SURGERY.

**BRYANT.** — A Manual for the Practice of
Surgery. By THOMAS BRYANT, F.R.C.S., Surgeon to, and Lecturer on
Surgery at, Guy's Hospital. Third Edition. With 672 Engravings
(nearly all original, many being coloured). 2 vols. Crown 8vo, 28s.

**BELLAMY.**—The Student's Guide to Surgical
Anatomy; a Text-Book for the Pass Examination. By EDWARD
BELLAMY, F.R.C.S., Surgeon to, and Lecturer on Anatomy and Practical
Surgery at, Charing Cross Hospital. With 50 Engravings. Fcap. 8vo,
6s. 6d.

**CLARK AND WAGSTAFFE.** — Outlines of
Surgery and Surgical Pathology. By F. LE GROS CLARK, F.R.C.S.,
F.R.S., Consulting Surgeon to St. Thomas's and the Great Northern
Hospitals. Second Edition. Revised and expanded by the Author,
assisted by W. W. WAGSTAFFE, F.R.C.S., Assistant-Surgeon to St.
Thomas's Hospital. 8vo, 10s. 6d.

**DRUITT.** — The Surgeon's Vade-Mecum; a
Manual of Modern Surgery. By ROBERT DRUITT, F.R.C.S. Eleventh
Edition. With 369 Engravings. Fcap. 8vo, 14s.

**FERGUSSON.**—A System of Practical Surgery.
By Sir WILLIAM FERGUSSON, Bart., F.R.C.S., F.R.S., late Surgeon and
Professor of Clinical Surgery to King's College Hospital. With 463
Engravings. Fifth Edition. 8vo, 21s.

**HEATH.**—A Manual of Minor Surgery and
Bandaging, for the use of House-Surgeons, Dressers, and Junior Practi-
tioners. By CHRISTOPHER HEATH, F.R.C.S., Holme Professor of Clinical
Surgery in University College and Surgeon to the Hospital. Fifth
Edition. With 83 Engravings. Fcap. 8vo, 5s. 6d.

*By the same Author.*

A Course of Operative Surgery: with
Twenty Plates drawn from Nature by M. LÉVEILLÉ, and Coloured
by hand under his direction. Large 8vo, 40s.

ALSO,

The Student's Guide to Surgical Diagnosis. Fcap. 8vo, 6s. 6d.

---

## SURGERY—*continued.*

*MAUNDER.*—Operative Surgery. By Charles
F. MAUNDER, F.R.C.S., late Surgeon to, and Lecturer on Surgery at,
the London Hospital. Second Edition. With 164 Engravings. Post
8vo, 6s.

*PIRRIE.*—The Principles and Practice of
Surgery. By WILLIAM PIRRIE, F.R.S.E., Professor of Surgery in the
University of Aberdeen. Third Edition. With 490 Engravings. 8vo, 28s.

## TERMINOLOGY.

*DUNGLISON.*—Medical Lexicon: a Dictionary
of Medical Science, containing a concise Explanation of its various
Subjects and Terms, with Accentuation, Etymology, Synonymes, &c.
By ROBLEY DUNGLISON, M.D. New Edition, thoroughly revised by
RICHARD J. DUNGLISON, M.D. Royal 8vo, 28s.

*MAYNE.*—A Medical Vocabulary: being an
Explanation of all Terms and Phrases used in the various Departments of Medical Science and Practice, giving their Derivation, Meaning,
Application, and Pronunciation. By ROBERT G. MAYNE, M.D., LL.D.,
and JOHN MAYNE, M.D., L.R.C.S.E. Fourth Edition. Fcap. 8vo, 10s.

## WOMEN, DISEASES OF.

*BARNES.*—A Clinical History of the Medical
and Surgical Diseases of Women. By ROBERT BARNES, M.D., F.R.C.P.,
Obstetric Physician to, and Lecturer on Diseases of Women, &c., at, St.
George's Hospital. Second Edition. With 181 Engravings. 8vo, 28s.

*DUNCAN.*—Clinical Lectures on Diseases of
Women. By J. MATTHEWS DUNCAN, M.D., Obstetric Physician to St.
Bartholomew's Hospital. 8vo.

*EMMET.* — The Principles and Practice of
Gynæcology. By THOMAS ADDIS EMMET, M.D., Surgeon to the
Woman's Hospital of the State of New York. With 130 Engravings.
Royal 8vo, 24s.

## WOMEN, DISEASES OF—*continued*.

*GALABIN.*—The Student's Guide to the Diseases of Women. By ALFRED L. GALABIN, M.D., F.R.C.P., Assistant Obstetric Physician and Joint Lecturer on Obstetric Medicine to Guy's Hospital. With 63 Engravings. Fcap. 8vo, 7s. 6d.

*SMITH.*—Practical Gynæcology: a Handbook of the Diseases of Women. By HEYWOOD SMITH, M.D., Physician to the Hospital for Women, and to the British Lying-in Hospital. With Engravings. Crown 8vo, 5s. 6d.

*WEST AND DUNCAN.*—Lectures on the Diseases of Women. By CHARLES WEST, M.D., F.R.C.P. Fourth Edition. Revised and in part re-written by the Author, with numerous additions, by J. MATTHEWS DUNCAN, M.D., Obstetric Physician to St. Bartholomew's Hospital. 8vo, 16s.

## ZOOLOGY.

*BRADLEY.*—Manual of Comparative Anatomy and Physiology. By S. MESSENGER BRADLEY, F.R.C.S., Lecturer on Practical Surgery in Owen's College, Manchester. Third Edition. With 61 Engravings. Post 8vo, 6s. 6d.

*CHAUVEAU AND FLEMING.*—The Comparative Anatomy of the Domesticated Animals. By A. CHAUVEAU, Professor at the Lyons Veterinary School; and GEORGE FLEMING. Veterinary Surgeon, Royal Engineers. With 450 Engravings. 8vo, 31s. 6d.

*HUXLEY.*—Manual of the Anatomy of Invertebrated Animals. By THOMAS H. HUXLEY, LL.D., F.R.S. With 156 Engravings. Fcap. 8vo, 16s.

*By the same Author.*

Manual of the Anatomy of Vertebrated Animals. With 110 Engravings. Post 8vo, 12s.

*WILSON.*—The Student's Guide to Zoology: a Manual of the Principles of Zoological Science. By ANDREW WILSON, Lecturer on Natural History, Edinburgh. With Engravings. Fcap. 8vo, 6s. 6d.

CPSIA information can be obtained at www.ICGtesting.com
Printed in the USA
LVOW131046250113

317068LV00005B/649/A